Bangla Ranna

An Introduction to Bengali Cuisine

Satarupa Banerjee

Orient BlackSwan

ORIENT BLACKSWAN PRIVATE LIMITED

Registered Office
3-6-752 Himayatnagar, Hyderabad 500 029 A.P. (India)
e-mail : centraloffice@orientblackswan.com

Other Offices
Bangalore, Bhopal, Bhubaneshwar, Chennai,
Ernakulam, Guwahati, Hyderabad, Jaipur, Kolkata,
Lucknow, Mumbai, New Delhi, Nodia, Patna

First Published by Orient Longman Private Limited 2006
First Orient Blackswan Impression 2013

Cover & book design

ISBN 978 81 250 2915 1

Printed in India at
Commercial Press Service, Kolkata-700 012

Published by
Orient Blackswan Private Limited
17, Chittaranjan Avenue, Kolkata-700 072
e-mail : kolkata@orientblackswan.com

Dedication

This book is for the countless housewives in Bengal who keep the tradition of Bengali cuisine alive.

Contents

Introduction

The roots of Bengali cuisine lie in a rural lifestyle that made extensive and innovative use of nature's bounty to produce exquisite delights from the simplest ingredients.

People's knowledge of food from west Bengal is restricted to 'maacher-jhol-bhat' (fish curry and rice), sandesh and rosogolla. There is, of course, a lot more. Far from being, as the rest of India thinks, just a cuisine that concentrates on fish, rice and mustard oil, Bengali cuisine with its subtle, delicate intermingling of flavours and the blend of the exotic with the ordinary, creates a gastronomical experience that can only be described as sheer bliss.

Cookery books written in Bengali have been in existence for more than a century . Notable among them are the tomes by Pragya Sundari Devi and Bipradas Mukhopadhyay. But these books do not contain only typically Bengali recipes. Pragya Sundari Devi's book comprises largely continental style of cooking and Bipradas's book relies heavily on Mughlai cuisine.

In Bengal, like in many other regions of India, recipes have been handed down from mother to daughter. The basic recipes are similar, but each family has its own variation, depending on the particular area it originally belonged to, and this version is always considered superior to anyone else's, of course!

Few communities can match the Bengalis in their love for good food and the care and skill with which they prepare it. Generally speaking, authentic, traditional Bengali food does not really lend itself to restaurant catering. So for a taste of the genuine stuff, you have to be invited to a Bengali home or you have to turn to this book.

The best Bengali food that you'll ever get will be in Bengali homes. People of no other culture spend such a disproportionately large part of their income on food as do the Bengalis. Extraordinarily expensive items like lobsters and hilsa get snapped up in no time. And the buyers are not affluent. Most of them are ordinary, middle class people, who take great pride in beating the others in getting the best, early in the morning.

One typical trait of the Bengalis is their habit of shopping every day. Most people prefer to buy fresh vegetables and fish despite the advances in refrigeration and other food-preservation techniques. Curiously, all the shopping is done by the men of the family and, for some, this is an addiction. Come morning and you'll see them on their way to the market with a plastic or jute shopping bag. The fish and vegetable market is also a meeting place to discuss the day's headlines or the latest cricket or football match. The men, most of whom have never seen the inside of a kitchen, know exactly which vegetables to buy for 'Shukto' (a vegetable medley with bitter gourd), or if they buy 'Mocha' (banana flower), that it must be accompanied by 'bori' (dry pellets made from a paste of pulses).

If you have managed to secure an invitation to lunch to taste pure, authentic 'Bangla ranna', let us see what you are in for. Bengalis, like their neighbours, the Oriyas, follow a certain sequence of dishes. You start with something bitter and then move through pungent, hot and sour or sweet sour dishes to the final delight of a sweet.

The meal begins with an 'uchche-charchari' a dry curry of bitter gourd eaten with rice and ghee; or 'shukto'—a dish of carefully blended vegetables, in which bitter gourd predominates. This is a recipe that Bengali mothers-in-law insist should be part of every daughter-in-law's repertoire of dishes. These are appetisers, which open up the taste buds and whet the appetite. This is followed by a dal and a 'bhaja' or some kind of fried vegetable. The dal is not as thick as the one served in northern India and is eaten with a dash of lime juice. Sometimes, a fish head or prawns are added. Dal can also be accompanied by other vegetarian dishes such as 'ghonto', made with pumpkin, colocassia stem and banana flower; or 'charchari', a combination of vegetables with a flavouring of 'paanch-phoran', the typical Bengali combination of five spices—aniseed, cumin, fengreek, nigella and radhuni, which resembles parsley seeds. Since radhuni is not available outside Bengal, ajwain can be used instead. Other vegetarian dishes served are the 'dalna' and the 'chokka'. All these dishes are cooked with different spices, seasonings and flavourings which are carefully chosen to enhance their natural taste.

The best vegetarian meals come from the kitchens of Bengali widows. Bengali widows of yesteryear (of course, things are changing now, though a few still follow the strict rules) never ate fish, meat, eggs, onion and garlic. Even masur dal was taboo, as it was supposed to be heat-inducing as was non-vegetarian food. So these widows created vegetarian masterpieces with a subtlety of spices that could transform even a mundane vegetable like radish or bottle gourd into an item of culinary bliss.

Bengalis are most particular about the way vegetables and fish are cut and use a razor-edged cutter called 'bonti', which has to be held down by the feet while seated. Though it requires some practice, the 'bonti' is versatile and can be used to cut vegetables, meat and fish to different specifications. Each course in Bengali cuisine demands a particularly way of cutting and chopping. For shukto, the vegetables must be sliced thin while dalna calls for chunkier pieces. For chorchori, a mixed vegetable dish, different vegetables are cut in different sizes and thickness as each cooks at a different pace. Care must be taken to avoid overcooking as the vegetables must retain their shape, colour and crispness.

It is difficult to imagine what Bengali food would be like without the ubiquitous banana and coconut. Just as our literature would be orphaned without Tagore, our cuisine would be insipid without the banana plant. We eat practically all parts of the banana plant. The fruit is eaten even before it ripens. The flower, called mocha, contains tiny unripe bananas within and cutting it is no mean feat as it takes both time and patience. Perhaps this is why busy housewives do not favour it any more. The purple cover of the flower is discarded and the rudiments of the bananas are cut into very tiny bits, soaked in water for some time and then cooked. The 'thod', the tender inner portion of the stem, requires elaborate cleaning and its fibres have to be carefully removed, sliced, and then cooked. Banana leaves are used as plates and we even cook fish in it. The strong fibres gathered from the outer barks are used to make small ropes and bags.

The coconut tree is equally vital to Bengali cuisine. The dry leaves are used as fuel in rural areas, while the thick veins of the leaves are cut and dried to make broomsticks. The unripe fruit serves as a first-rate thirst quencher, while the ripe ones need no introduction. The ultimate in Bengali cuisine is a special prawn dish in which prawns and certain spices are put inside a tender coconut which is then plastered with mud and roasted over a fire. The coconut flesh and water blend with the prawns, producing an exquisitely-flavoured delicacy.

Fish occupies the pride of place in any Bengali meal, ordinary or festive. If he could afford it, a Bengali would have fish for lunch and dinner and would not be averse to having a piece of fried fish for breakfast as well! He will go to any lengths to procure good quality fish for an honoured guest, never mind the cost. It is one of the idiosycracies of the Bengalis that sea food is not favoured, the only exceptions being prawns and crabs. With so many large rivers, ponds, tanks and marshes, there is no dearth of freshwater fish like rui, katla, chitol, pabda, parshe, tangra, etc. Fish is cooked in every possible way – boiled, steamed, roasted, fried and curried – invariably in mustard oil, sometimes with vegetables, using different spices, seasonings and flavourings.

Then there are the fish dishes with hilsa or ilish mach as the Bengalis call it. Found in the delta waters in Bengal, the seasonal arrival of hilsa is an occasion for celebration. You have to be a Bengali or a cat to enjoy hilsa. Others find it difficult to tackle the myriad minute bones. And yet, the creamy texture of this special fish is a treat worth waiting for. A delicious curry with hilsa, ginger, turmeric, green chilli and nigella can be made within minutes. The fish head also plays a crucial role in traditional Bengali cuisine. Dry roasted mung dal with fish head, called murtighonto, is a delicacy. The fish head is also cooked with bottle gourd or cabbage as a dry dish. Other bones and parts of the large rohu or carp are used to make chanchra along with vegetables. Another traditional dish is a sort of biryani with fish head and rice. In fact, one could write a whole book on cooking fish the Bengali way.

A strange phenomenon of Bengali cuisine is that the repertoire of meat dishes is limited, in spite of the extensive Muslim and British influences. We have been eating mutton and chicken for a long time but preparation of elaborate meat dishes has never been our forte, though a meat curry is invariably included in the menu. Traditional Bengali homes normally cook a meat curry once a week. Called mangshor jhol, this is a light and fragrant curry, rather like a stew. The other popular meat preparation is mangshor chop, a great favourite at weddings. This is essentially a potato cutlet with a mince filling. East Bengali Muslim cuisine has many delicious meat dishes including biryani and many different kababs. One speciality is a white meat curry, called Rezala, made with yogurt, onions, garlic, ginger and whole garam masala.

As the meal draws to a close, a chutney is served. Sweet and sour chutneys are an essential part of a Bengali meal and the ingredients depend on the season—raw mango, pineapple, tomato, green olive, green papaya, or again fish, and even rosogolla. These chutneys are sweetened with sugar or jaggery.

A Bengali meal, however exotic or simple, invariably ends with sweets, as we are extraordinarily fond of them. A Bengali will gladly travel from one end of the city to the other to buy a particular sweet from a particular shop if he feels it is made better there than elsewhere.

Bengali sweets, usually made from casein, are unparalleled in their variety and delicacy of taste. They are not too sweet. Hardly any artificial colouring or preservatives are used, which makes them easily digestible and nutritious. The most popular sweets are sandesh and rosogolla.

Bengal's best emissary after Rabindranath Tagore and Satyajit Ray, the round syrupy rosogolla, needs no introduction. With its history of more than a century, the rosogolla has crossed the boundaries of caste, culture and creed. It was invented in 1868 in a tiny sweet shop at Bagbazar in North Kolkata. Its creator, Nabin Chandra Das, was desparate to invent a new sweet that could compete with the 'Sandesh'. He endeavoured to create a sweet that was soft and succulent against the dry texture of the sandesh. He did succeed, although after initial failures. It is interesting to note that the 'rosogolla' did not gain instant popularity. In fact, it was several years before it found favour with the Bengalis. Later, it was Nabin Chandra's son, better known as K. C. Das, who promoted its sale in India and abroad by making its tinned variety available. And this confection, like the Kalighat and Howrah Bridge, has become an inherent part of Kolkata.

The other sweet firmly entrenched in Bengali hearts is the sandesh. Sandesh can he made in over 100 different flavours and textures. The general demarcation in the texture would be the hard or the 'karapak' and the soft or the 'narampak' sandesh. The former variety keeps better and is preferred if it is to be carried over a long distance. The latter has a shorter shelf-life and refrigeration spoils the taste. Kamala sandesh, flavoured with grated orange peel, has a special attraction. A traditional flavouring agent is the Khejur gur or date-palm jaggery. This jaggery is seasonal and is available only during winter. The jaggery is obtained by tapping the juice of the date-palm tree (just as maple syrup is obtained from the maple tree). The juice is collected and boiled down to make liquid jaggery or solidified into a round block, called *patali*. It has a delicious flavour and imparts a distinctive taste and colour to sweet dishes.

There are other sweets almost as good, like the langcha, pantua (Bengal's answer to the gulab jamun) or the more renowned Lady Kenny, created to celebrate the birthday of lady Canning, wife of the then Governor General. Then there are the sweets particular to different regions, such as sarbhaja and sarpuria from Krishnanagar, both made from the creamy layer that forms on top of the milk, boiled on low heat; sitabhog and mihidana of Burdwan and moya-laddus of sweetened kheel, of Jayanagar. Another sweet unique to Bengal is mishti doi or sweet yoghurt, usually available in shops, where it is made in earthen pots of different sizes.

There are a few sweets – collectively called pithe – which are made at home and cannot be easily bought. These also include different kinds of payesh or kheers. They are made with rice, pressed rice, coconut and jaggery.

A discussion of Bengali food would be incomplete without a mention being made of the two different styles of cooking in the state—the ghoti (belonging to West Bengal) and the bangal from erstwhile East Bengal, now Bangladesh. Though the migrant East Bengalis have made West Bengal their home and the two cultures have integrated, a lot of rivalry and bantering continues. Historically speaking, West Bengal's fertile soil ensured that crops grew easily and, thus, people had more time to pursue cultural activities. However, in East Bengal, recurrent floods made life difficult. People found it hard to move out of their homes when the rivers were in flood and this is reflected in their food habits. For instance, they had to rely on dehydrated fish called shutki mach. The bangals deride ghoti food as cloyingly sweet, bland without much oil and spices. 'What do the ghotis know of good cooking, anyhow?' they say. On their part, the ghotis decry the bangal way of eating 'foul smelling' shutki fish and drowning their food in too much oil and spices. 'The bangals even put fish in their shukto, can you believe it?' they exclaim! I must be one of the very few thoroughbred ghotis who love bangal food, minus the shutki mach, of course!

Traditional Bengali wedding feasts used to be memorable. The meal used to be served on glistening banana leaves. The first course consisted of fried brinjals, lentils with fish head, a dalna with seasonal vegetables with luchi or radha-ballabhi (dal-stuffed puries). This was followed by pulao or ghee bhat (rice cooked in a little ghee, a very light kind of pulao), served with at least two kinds of fish and one of mutton. Dahi fish, prawn malaikari and mustard hilsa were great favourites. Green mangoes, when in season, were always preferred for the chutney, which came next. Heading the sweet list would be mishti doi and this is such a favourite. The choice of sweets was always so wide that one was seldom offered the same sweet twice in the course of a marriage season.

Unfortunately, times have changed. Modern life, with all its hustle and bustle, has taken its toll. Wedding feasts have been transformed with the emergence of the professional caterers. Menus have also undergone a change as the Bengali palate has expanded to accept non-Bengali cuisine. In recent times, dishes like Kashmiri aloo dum, navratan pulao, Amritsari machi, biryani, tandoori chicken, naan, fish butter fry, chole bhature and even chilli fish feature more often. What really pains me is that ice cream has replaced sweet yoghurt more often than not, though I must admit, judging by my daughter's reaction, this seems to have gone down most favourably with the younger generation. The mode of service has also changed. Seldom do you find banana leaves and earthenware glasses these days. Now you are served by uniformed bearers on laminated tables in china crockery. An era has certainly ended but the Bengali passion for food continues.

Abbreviations

gm	–	gram
kg	–	kilogram
lt	–	litre
ml	–	millilitre
tsp	–	teaspoon
tbsp	–	tablespoon

Weights & Measures

Recipes in this book use the standard measuring cups and spoons.
A graduated set of four cups measuring 1 cup, ½ cup, ⅓ cup and ¼ cup.
A graduated set of 4 spoons measuring 1 tablespoon, 1 teaspoon, ½ teaspoon and ¼ teaspoon.
1 tablespoon is equal to 3 teaspoons.

All measurements are level unless otherwise stated.

Liquids: Place the measuring cup on a flat surface and pour the liquid to the required level. The spoons should also be filled to the level.

Dry Ingredients: These should be spooned lightly into the cup until heaped, then levelled off with a straight edged knife or spatula.

Never pack the ingredients down or shake or tap the cup. And, unless specified, measure before sifting.

Rice Dishes

Ghee Bhat (Light Pulao)
Macher Pulao (Fish Pulao)
Bhuni Khichuri (Pulao-like Khichri)

Ghee Bhat

Light Pulao

SERVE 6

Preparation time	:	½ hour for soaking the rice
Cooking time	:	25 minutes

Most of the fish dishes that we cook go very well with plain boiled rice, but I don't lik to serve plain rice when cooking for company. This simple pulao comes in very handy then.

INGREDIENTS

Basmati rice	~	*½ kg*
Saffron	~	*¼ tsp*
Warm milk	~	*2 tbsp*
Ghee	~	*5 tbsp*
Whole cashewnuts	~	*20*
Raisins	~	*2 handfuls*
Green cardamoms	~	*4*
Cinnamon	~	*5 cm piece*
Hot water	~	*1 lt*
Salt	~	*to taste*
Sugar	~	*2 tbsp*
Ginger juice	~	*1 tsp*

- Pick, wash and soak the rice for half an hour.
- If you are using saffron, soak it in milk. Keep aside.
- In 1 tablespoon of ghee, lightly fry the cashewnuts and raisins and set aside.
- In a heavy bottomed 'degchi', heat the remaining ghee, put in the slightly crushed cardamoms and cinnamon.
- When the spices turn a shade darker, add the drained rice, stirring for 3–4 minutes or until the rice acquires a parched look (until it starts to look opaque).
- Add the hot water, salt, sugar, ginger juice, cashewnuts and raisins.
- Bring to a boil. Cover, reduce heat to very low and cook till the water reduces to the level of the rice and holes appear on its surface.
- Uncover, mix the rice very lightly with a fork. Sprinkle the saffron milk all over.
- Cover and cook again, placing a tawa underneath the degchi. Cook till the rice is done.
- Serve hot.

Macher Pulao

Fish Pulao

SERVES 6

Preparation time : 20 minutes
Cooking time : 1 hour

Bhetki or hilsa can be substituted for rohu, but the fish must be large. In Bengal, we call it 'paka mach', that is, mature fish.

INGREDIENTS

Almonds	~	*10*	*Onion*	~	*2*
Basmati rice	~	*2 cups*	*Green cardamom*	~	*3*
Rohu fish	~	*½ kg*	*Bay leaves*	~	*3*
Onion paste	~	*2 tbsp*	*Saffron*	~	*1 pinch*
Garlic paste	~	*1 tsp*	*Ginger paste*	~	*1 tsp*
Salt	~	*to taste*	*Milk*	~	*to soak saffron*
Refined oil	~	*½ cup*			*in sugar-2 tsp*
Ghee	~	*2 tbsp*			*(optional)*

- Blanch the almonds. Pick and wash the rice.
- Cut the fish into 10 pieces. Mix the fish with onion paste, half the garlic paste and ½ a teaspoon of salt. Keep aside for 15 minutes.
- Heat oil in a karahi. Gently fry the fish, 5 pieces at a time, till light brown. Take out and reserve.
- Heat ghee in a heavy bottomed degchi. Add chopped onions. Fry till they just turn transparent, but are still soft.
- Add the garlic paste. Stir fry for a minute.
- Add the almonds, cardamoms and bay leaves and stir.
- Add the rice and ginger paste and fry for 3 minutes or till they look parched.
- Stir in 4 cups of hot water and salt to taste. You may also add 2 teaspoons of sugar. Instead of water, chicken stock may also be used.
- Cover the vessel. When the rice comes to a boil, lower the heat.
- When water reduces to the level of the rice and you find holes appearing on the surface, place the fish pieces over the rice. Pour any oil left over from frying fish. Cover and let it cook for 5 minutes. Add saffron mixed with milk.
- Put on *dum*. This means putting a tawa underneath the degchi. Cook thus till the rice is done and fluffy. This should take at least 20 minutes. The pulao may be finished in an oven, too.

- Garnish with fried potatoes, if desired.
- Serve with any curry with gravy.

Note: ½ a teaspoon of turmeric can be used in place of saffron.

Bhuni Khichuri

Pulao-like Khichri

SERVES 6

Preparation time : 10 minutes
Cooking time : 1 hour

A khichri with almost pulao-like consistency. Try it—it is party fare. The mutton may be prepared beforehand and used when needed.

INGREDIENTS

For the meat:

Mutton	~	*½ kg*
Mustard oil	~	*2 tbsp*
Ghee	~	*1 tbsp*
Salt	~	*to taste*
Grind to a paste		
Onion	~	*1, large*
Ginger	~	*2.5 cm piece*
Garlic	~	*4 cloves*
Green cardamoms	~	*2*
Cloves	~	*2.5 cm long stick*
Cumin seed	~	*1 tsp*
Coriander seed	~	*1 tsp*
Poppy seed	~	*1 tbsp*
Tomatoes	~	*2, large*
Dry red chillies	~	*2*

Turmeric	~	*½ tsp*	*Turmeric*	~	*1 tsp*
For the khichri:			*Salt*	~	*to taste*
Basmati rice	~	*250 g*	*Sugar*	~	*1 tsp*
Ghee	~	*2 tbsp*	*Cashewnuts*	~	*15*
Bay leaves	~	*2*	*Raisins*	~	*25*
Mung dal	~	*125 g*			

For the meat:

- The meat must be cut into small pieces.
- Heat the mustard oil to smoking point; add ghee.
- Once the ghee melts, add the ground paste and fry over medium heat, stirring frequently till the oil surfaces.
- Add the mutton and salt and stir fry till the moisture from the meat dries up.
- Add just enough water to cover meat and cook till done. A pressure cooker may be used at this stage. Let excess liquid, if any, evaporate.

For the khichri:

- Heat ghee in a 'degchi'. Season with bay leaves.

- When they change colour, add mung dal. Stir fry till you get a fried aroma and the dal starts to pick up brown spots.
- Add turmeric, salt, sugar, cashewnuts, raisins, 750 ml hot water and rice. Cover. When it comes to a boil, reduce the heat. Stir the rice a few times in between.
- When the water goes down to the level of the rice, add the cooked mutton. Stir to mix lightly and put on *dum*.
- You can do this either by placing a tawa beneath the degchi or by placing the degchi over a pan of simmering water.
- Cook till the rice is done. The rice may break, but that's all right.
- Serve with dollops of butter and papads.

Fish Dishes

Jamai Bhog (Prawns in Green Coconut Shell)

Smoked Hilsa

Macher Hingli (Fish with Raisins)

Macher Shanta (Fish with Almonds)

Tel Koi (Climbing Perch in Mustard Oil)

Aam Shole (Fish with Green Mango)

Macher Kalia Phool Kopi Diye (Fish and Cauliflower Curry)

(Continues. . . .)

Chitol Macher Muitha (Fish Dumpling Curry)

Kankrar Jhal (Crab Curry)

Macher Dum (Fish Curry)

Macher Chatni (Fish Chutney)

Posto Mach (Fish with Poppy Seeds)

Ilish Macher Paturi (Hilsa Fish in Banana Leaves)

Lau Chingri (Prawns with Bottle Gourd)

Macher Kosturi (Fish in Milk)

Shorshe Pomfret (Pomfret with Mustard)

(Continues. . .)

Matarshutir Mach (Fish with Peas)

Koi Macher Hara Gouri (Fish with two kinds of Sauce)

Adar Mach (Fish with Ginger)

Macher Jhuro (Dry Fish Curry)

Macher Kabri (Fish with Milk and Butter)

Macher Tak Jhal (Sour Fish Curry)

Topse Mach Bhaja (Topse Fish Fry)

Macher Chorchori (Fish Dry Curry)

Chingri Macher Shalmi (Prawns with Tamarind)

Jamai Bhog

Prawns in Green Coconut Shell

SERVES 4

Preparation time : 30 minutes
Cooking time : 50 minutes

A culinary marvel—no wonder it is called 'son-in-law's special'! Traditionally, the coconut was roasted on coal embers. Now, we bake it. Have the outer husk of the green coconut removed, as far as possible; the coconut seller will do it for you. This will enable you to fit it in the oven and also shorten the baking time.

INGREDIENTS

Green coconut	~	*1*
Tiger prawns	~	*½ kg*
Mustard paste	~	*2 tbsp*
Turmeric	~	*½ tbsp*
Green chillies	~	*4*
Salt	~	*to taste*
Mustard oil	~	*2 tbsp*

- Ensure that the green coconut has some tender meat. Cut a portion off the top of the coconut. Keep aside. Discard the coconut water.
- Shell and devein the prawns. You may keep the heads on or discard them—it's up to you.
- Mix the prawns with the rest of the ingredients.
- Spoon the prawn mixture into the coconut. Fix the top portion of the coconut on with atta dough.
- Preheat the oven to 400°F / 200°C. Bake the coconut in it for 45–50 minutes.
- Break the top open and take out prawns along with the coconut meat, which should also be cooked soft.
- Serve hot with rice.

Smoked Hilsa

SERVES 4

Preparation time : 20 minutes +marination

Cooking time : 25 minutes

A very modern Bengali dish, obviously influenced by the Western smoked fish. This highly expensive 5-star recipe can be easily prepared at home and at a much lower cost. This is how. . .

INGREDIENTS

Hilsa fish, whole	~	*1½ kg*
Malt vinegar	~	*¾ cup*
Salt	~	*to taste*
Onion	~	*400 g*
Ginger	~	*100 g*
Limes	~	*2*
Kashmiri chilli powder	~	*1 tsp*
Butter	~	*1 tbsp*

Garnish

Lemon slices

Onion slices

Tomato wedges

- Scale the whole fish, removing the head and tail; clean the innards. Remove the two fillets from the sides, but retain the skin. Halve each fillet vertically.
- Marinate the fish in a solution of vinegar and salt for 6 hours, turning over the fish a few times in between.
- Remove the fish from the marinade; wipe dry. Press the fish from one side and take out the larger bones; they will come out easily. Take out as many bones as you can.
- Grind onion and ginger and extract the juice.
- Marinate the fish again for an hour in onion-ginger juice, lime juice, chilli powder and salt.
- Grease a baking dish with butter and lay the fish fillets on it. Do not overlap. If necessary, do it in batches.
- Take an aluminium pot. Grease and put 4 tablespoons of sugar in it.
- Preheat over to 400°F / 200°C. Place the pot with the sugar on the lowest rack and the tray containing fish just above it. Close the oven and allow the fumes to accumulate.
- Check fish once by piercing it with a needle. It is done if the stick comes out clean. If not, bake till done. Do not open the oven door unnecessarily or else the fumes will escape and the fish will lose its smoky flavour.

- You may further slice the fish lengthwise and take out the minute bones. But in any case, these bones are so soft that they pose no problem. Piece them together before serving.
- Serve garnished with slices of lemon, and onion and tomato wedges.

Note: You can get the fish seller to fillet the fish for you.

Macher Hingli

Fish with Raisins

SERVES 4

Preparation time : 5 minutes
Cooking time : 20 minutes

This is best cooked with 'magur' fish. But 'magur' being very expensive, rohu or 'telapia' can be substituted.

INGREDIENTS

Magur fish	~ *½ kg*	*Asafoetida*	~ *A pinch*
Raisins	~ *200 g*	*Ginger paste*	~ *1½ tsp*
Mustard oil	~ *2 tbsp*	*Chilli powder*	~ *½ tsp*
Ghee	~ *2 tbsp*	*Curd*	~ *2 tbsp*
Bay leaves	~ *2*	*Salt*	~ *to taste*
Peppercorns	~ *10*	*Sugar*	~ *1 tsp*

- Wash the fish well and cut into fairly large pieces.
- Grind the raisins to a coarse paste.
- Heat mustard oil in a karahi till it starts smoking; add ghee. Temper with bay leaves and peppercorns. Once they stop spluttering, add the asafoetida.
- Mix the raisin paste, ginger paste and chilli powder with ¼ cup of water and add to the oil in the karahi.
- Fry over a medium heat for 3 minutes. Add well-beaten curd and stir fry for another 2 minutes.
- Add fish and fry for another couple of minutes.
- Add 1 cup of water, salt and sugar.
- Cook till the fish is done, and the moisture has almost evaporated and the oil floats on top.
- There should be a thick gravy clinging to the fish.
- Serve with rice or pulao.

Macher Shanta

Fish with Almonds

SERVES 6

Preparation time : 15 minutes
Cooking time : 5 minutes

Rather expensive, but well worth it. Use rohu, kotla, bhetki or koi.

INGREDIENTS

Fish	~	*½ kg*	*Green cardamoms*	~	*2*
Almonds	~	*25*	*Cinnamon*	~	*2½ cm stick*
Onion	~	*3*	*Cloves*	~	*2*
Green chillies	~	*2*	*Bay leaves*	~	*2*
Ginger	~	*2½ cm piece*	*Sugar*	~	*1 tbsp*
Curd	~	*3 tbsp*	*Salt*	~	*to taste*
Ghee	~	*2 tbsp*	*Lime juice*	~	*1 tsp*

- Wash and dry the fish. Blanch and peel the almonds.
- Blend the almonds, onions, green chillies, ginger and curd in a mixer till smooth.
- Heat ghee in a karahi. Temper with cardamoms, cinnamon and cloves, slightly bruised, and bay leaves.
- Add the blended masala, fish, sugar and salt. Mix well. No water is to be added.
- Transfer this to a tightly-covered container and steam in a pressure cooker for 7 minutes.
- Sprinkle with lime juice and serve. This has a sweetish taste, with just a hint of sourness.
- Serve with plain ghee bhat.

Tel Koi

Climbing Perch in Mustard Oil

SERVES 4

Preparation time : 10 minutes
Cooking time : 30 minutes

As the name itself suggests, the main ingredient of this dish, besides fish, is mustard oil. So for this, you need a little more than the usual quantity of oil. Telapia may be substituted, for 'Koi' is not always readily available.

INGREDIENTS

Koi fish	~	*½ kg*	*Onion paste*	~	*1 cup*
Turmeric	~	*1 tsp*	*Ginger paste*	~	*1½ tsp*
Salt	~	*to taste*	*Cumin powder*	~	*1 tsp*
Mustard oil	~	*150 ml*	*Chilli powder*	~	*1 tsp*
Whole cuminseeds	~	*¾ tsp*	*Tomato, large*	~	*1*
Bay leaves	~	*2*			

- Clean the fish, but keep them whole. Smear with half the turmeric and ½ a teaspoon of salt.
- Heat oil in a karahi, lightly fry the fish and take them out. You will have to do this in batches.
- Temper the same oil with cumin seeds and bay leaves.
- When these stop spluttering, add the onion paste and stir fry.
- Once the onion turns pink, add the ginger paste, cumin powder, chilli powder and turmeric and stir fry till the oil separates. Sprinkle 1 tablespoon of water.
- Add the chopped tomato, and stir till it turns soft, sprinkling a little water, to prevent the spices getting burnt.
- Add the fish, 1 cup of water and salt.
- Cover and cook till the fish is done. Uncover and cook till the moisture evaporates and the oil surfaces. There should be a very thick gravy.
- Serve with rice.

Aam Shole

Fish with Green Mango

SERVES 4

Preparation time : 5 minutes
Cooking time : 25 minutes

In Bengal, we use what is known as 'shole' fish. It is somewhat like 'Seer' fish.

INGREDIENTS

Shole or seer fish	~	*750 g*	*Turmeric*	~	*1 tsp*
Small green mangoes	~	*2*	*Paanch phoran*	~	*1½ tsp*
Mustard oil	~	*¾ cup*	*Sugar*	~	*1 tbsp*
Salt	~	*to taste*			

- Discard the skin and bones of the fish and cut it into chunks. Or, get the fish seller to do it for you.
- Peel the mangoes and cut into slivers. Roast and powder 1 teaspoon of paanch phoran.

- Heat the oil in a karahi till it starts smoking. Smear the fish with ½ a teaspoon salt and ½ a teaspoon of turmeric. Add to the hot oil and fry lightly. Set aside.
- Temper the oil left in karahi with the rest of the paanch phoran.
- When the spices pop add the mango pieces and salt. Stir for one minute.
- Add the turmeric and fish. Fry for another 2 minutes carefully so as not to break the fish.
- Add sugar and one cup of water. Allow it to cook for 10 minutes.
- When the oil starts to float on top, sprinkle the powdered paanch phoran and remove.
- Serve with rice.

Macher Kalia Phool Kopi Diye

SERVES 6

Fish and Cauliflower Curry

Preparation time : 15 minutes
Cooking time : 35 minutes

This used to be a winter delicacy we looked forward to. Now, with cauliflower available all the year round, the dish is yours for the asking. This is particularly good with rohu, tangra or bhetki.

INGREDIENTS

Fish	~	*750 g*	*Whole cumin seeds*	~	*1 tsp*
Turmeric	~	*1 tsp*	*Sugar*	~	*½ tsp*
Salt	~	*to taste*	*Ginger paste*	~	*2 tsp*
Mustard oil	~	*1 cup*	*Chilli powder*	~	*1 tsp*
Potatoes, medium	~	*200 g*	*Coriander powder*	~	*1 tsp*
Cauliflower, medium	~	*1*	*Pepper powder*	~	*½ tsp*
Tomatoes, large	~	*2*	*Curd*	~	*3 tbsp*

Shelled green peas	~	*1 cup*	*Garam masala powder*	~	*1 tsp*
Pure ghee	~	*1 tbsp*			

- Wash and smear the fish with a little turmeric and salt.
- Heat oil in a karahi till it starts to smoke; add the fish, 4–5 pieces at a time. Deep fry till they turn a light golden-brown. Remove and reserve.
- Peel and cube the potatoes. Divide the cauliflower into florets. Chop the tomatoes.
- In the same oil, fry the potatoes and cauliflower separately till lightly coloured. Keep aside.
- Remove all but 2–3 tablespoons of oil from the karahi. Temper with whole cumin seeds.
- When they stop spluttering, add the sugar. When it caramelises, add the ginger paste, turmeric, chilli, coriander, cumin, pepper powder mixed with ¼ cup of water. Stir till the water evaporates.
- Add the tomato. Fry, stirring, till it softens.
- Add well-beaten curd, a little at a time, stirring continually. When all the curd is used up and the oil separates, add potatoes, cauliflower and peas.
- Stir fry for a minute and add 3 cups of water. Cover and cook till the vegetables are almost done.
- Add the fish and allow it to cook till done. There should be a medium-thick gravy.
- Add ghee and garam masala powder and serve.

Chitol Macher Muitha

Fish Dumpling Curry

SERVES 6

Prepartion time : 3 minutes
Cooking time : 30 minutes

A speciality of East Bengal cuisine. It is cooked only with 'Chitol' or 'Morh' fish. Buy the back portion and not the belly of the fish. In this recipe, only the upper portion of the fish is used and not the belly part. If you take a piece of fish in your hand you can easily see the bone. You have to scrape alongside the bones so you have only the flesh in your spoon and the bones remain attached to the skin.

INGREDIENTS

Back portion of Chitol fish	~	*½ kg*	*Salt*	~	*to taste*
Potatoes	~	*250 g*	*Mustard oil*	~	*1 cup*
Tomatoes, large	~	*2*	*Bay leaves*	~	*2*
Chilli powder	~	*1½ tsp*	*Cloves*	~	*4*

Green cardamoms	~	*4*	*Turmeric*	~	*1 tsp*
Cinnamon	~	*5 cm stick*	*Ghee*	~	*1 tbsp*
Onions, large	~	*3*	*Garam masala powder*	~	*1 tsp*
Ginger paste	~	*2 tsp*			

- Wash and cut the fish lengthwise into 3 pieces; scrape the fish with a spoon with the bones and not against them. You will find most of the bones will remain stuck to the skin. Remove the few still left in the flesh.
- Boil two small potatoes; peel and mash. Grind the onion; chop tomatoes.
- Combine the mashed potatoes, fish, ½ teaspoon of chilli powder, ½ a teaspoon of salt, 2 tablespoons of mustard oil.
- Mix well. Take a handful of the fish mixture and roll in your palms till smooth. Now, press it with your fist to give a dented shape. Prepare the others in the same way.
- Heat enough water in a large pan. When it comes to a boil, add the fish balls carefully. Turn once in between. When done they will rise to the surface.
- Take out with a perforated spoon and let them cool. Cut into thick slices and fry in hot oil. Set aside.
- Peel and cut the remaining potatoes into cubes. Lightly fry, using the same oil in which the fish was fried; set aside.

- Using the same oil, heat 3 tablespoons in a karahi. Season with bay leaves and whole garam masala.
- When they turn a shade darker, add the ground onion, tomatoes, turmeric, ginger paste and chilli powder, stir frying after each addition. Fry for 3 minutes.
- Add 2 cups of water, potatoes and salt. Cover and cook over medium heat.
- When the potatoes are almost done, add the fried fish pieces. Let them cook for 5 minutes.
- Add garam masala powder and ghee and remove.

Note: The fried fish cubes can be eaten as a snack, too.

Kankrar Jhal

Crab Curry

SERVES 4

Preparation time : 15 minutes
Cooking time : 25 minutes

'Kankra' or crabs are immensely popular in Bengal. Crabs are invariably sold alive. Never buy dead ones. The fish seller will kill them and crack the claws for you.

Now, proceed this way. Wash the claws, legs and body, scrubbing the shells thoroughly. Discard the stomach bag attached to the shell below the eyes. Also throw away the greyish-white-spongy, fern-like matter. Crack the claws and the small legs.The meat can be picked or left in the shells.

INGREDIENTS

Crabs	~	*4*	*Mustard oil*	~	*75 ml*
Ginger	~	*2 cm piece*	*Onion, large*	~	*1*
Garlic	~	*6 cloves*	*Turmeric*	~	*½ tsp*

Chilli powder	~	*1 tsp*
Salt	~	*to taste*
Mustard paste	~	*2 tbsp*
Green chillies	~	*4*

- Clean as directed and soak the crabs in saline water for half an hour.
- Grind the ginger and garlic.
- Heat oil in a karahi. Add the chopped onion, and sauté for 2–3 minutes.
- Add the ground paste, turmeric, and chilli powder. Fry well on a low flame till the oil separates and the spices are a light brown.
- Put in the drained crabs and salt. Stir fry for a couple of minutes on medium heat or until the crabs have turned red.
- Add the mustard paste, slit green chillies and ¼ cup of water.
- Bring to a boil. Cover and simmer for 10 minutes or until crabs are cooked.
- Serve with rice.

Macher Dum

Fish Curry

SERVES 6

Preparation time : 10 minutes
Cooking time : 20 minutes

INGREDIENTS

Fish	~	*1 kg*
Onions	~	*2 large*
Ginger	~	*2½ cm piece*
Dry red chillies	~	*4*
Garlic	~	*4 cloves*
Curd	~	*250 ml*
Nutmeg	~	*¼*
Mace	~	*1 petal*
Cloves	~	*2*
Cinnamon	~	*2 cm stick*
Green cardamom	~	*2*
Raisins	~	*20*
Cashewnuts	~	*10*
Mustard oil	~	*100 ml*
Bay leaves	~	*2*
Peppercorns	~	*10*
Sugar	~	*1 tbsp*
Turmeric	~	*1 tsp*
Salt	~	*to taste*

- Grind the onion, ginger, garlic and dry red chillies together in the mixer. Add the curd and blend again. Reserve.
- Dry-grind the nutmeg, mace, cloves, cinnamon and green cardamom together. Set aside.
- Grind the raisins and cashewnuts together.
- Heat oil in a degchi till smoking. Temper it with bay leaves and peppercorns.
- Add sugar. Let it caramelise.
- Add the ground onion paste and turmeric. Cook, stirring continually, till it turns brownish in colour.
- Add the fish, 1 cup of hot water, salt and raisin-cashew paste. Mix well.
- When it comes to a boil, cover and reduce the heat.
- Cook till the fish is done and the gravy considerably reduced.
- Add the dry ground spices and remove.
- Serve hot with rice or pulao.

Macher Chatni

Fish Chutney

SERVES 6

Preparation time : 10 minutes
Cooking time : 15 minutes

If you've never tasted fish chutney before, do try. You'll love it. Any of the following fish will do—hilsa, prawn, rohu or even fish roe.

INGREDIENTS

Fish	~	*250 g*
Salt	~	*¼ tsp*
Turmeric	~	*a pinch*
Mustard oil	~	*½ cup*
Mustard seeds	~	*1 tsp*
Dry red chilli	~	*1*
Tamarind paste	~	*2 tbsp*
Jaggery	~	*½ cup*
Roasted paanch-phoran powder	~	*2 tsp*

- Wash and cut the fish or roe into small pieces.

- Smear the fish with salt and turmeric and deep fry till golden-brown in the case of hilsa or rohu. Lightly fry in the case of prawns and roe. Keep aside.
- Mix the tamarind paste and jaggery with 1 ½ cups of water.
- Heat 2 tablespoons of oil in a karahi. Temper with mustard seeds and dry red chilli.
- When it stops spluttering, add the tamarind mix.
- Put in the fish and cook for 10 minutes. By this time, the gravy will also thicken.
- Sprinkle roasted paanch phoran powder and remove.
- Serve at room temperature.

Posto Mach

SERVES 4

Fish with Poppy Seeds

Preparation time : 10 minutes
Cooking time : 30 minutes

Poppy seeds are used in Bengali cooking at the drop of a hat; this spice does make a lot of difference to the taste and texture of a dish.

INGREDIENTS

Rohu or tangra fish	~	*½ kg*	*Garlic*	~	*4 cloves*
Mustard oil	~	*100 ml*	*Potatoes*	~	*250 g*
Poppy seeds	~	*100 g*	*Turmeric*	~	*a pinch*
Green chillies	~	*6*	*Salt*	~	*to taste*

- Cut rohu fish into small pieces. If using tangra, keep it whole.
- Grind the poppy seeds with 2 green chillies. Peel and cube potatoes.

- Heat oil in a karahi. Fry the fish smeared with a little salt till it is golden-brown. Remove.
- In the same oil, add the chopped garlic and fry till brown.
- Add the potatoes and fry till a light brown.
- Add slit green chillies, poppy seed paste and turmeric. Keep stirring on medium heat till it is lightly coloured. Add 1 cup of water and salt.
- Put in the fish and cover.
- Cook till the potatoes are done. Let excess liquid, if any, evaporate.
- This is rather a dry dish, but it goes well with rice.

Ilish Macher Paturi

SERVES 6

Hilsa Fish in Banana Leaves

Prepartion time : 10 minutes + 1 hour marination

Cooking time : 15 minutes

This reminds one of the 'patrani machhi' of the Parsis.

INGREDIENTS

Hilsa fish	~	*12 pieces*	*Turmeric*	~	*¾ tsp*
Black mustard seeds	~	*1 tbsp*	*Mustard oil*	~	*2 tbsp*
Yellow mustard seeds	~	*1½ tbsp*	*Salt*	~	*to taste*
Green chillies	~	*4*	*Banana leaves*	~	*12 pieces*
Coconut	~	*½*			

- Grate the coconut and grind it along with both kinds of mustard seeds and green chillies.

- Mix the ground paste, turmeric, mustard oil and salt together; smear the fish with it and marinate for 1 hour.
- Wrap each piece of fish in a clean banana leaf. Fold the leaf over the fish to cover it well. Tie each package securely with a piece of string.
- There are various ways of cooking this. It can be steamed in a pressure cooker for 10 minutes, or baked in a hot oven (400°F / 200°C) for 15–20 minutes. Or you can roast them on a lightly oiled tawa till the leaves turn reddish. What Bengalis do is to put the packets in the rice immediately after straining; the heat of the rice cooks the fish.
- Sometimes the fish is also wrapped in tender pumpkin or bottle gourd leaves and left in the hot rice to cook, thus making an edible packet.

Lau Chingri

SERVES 4

Prawns with Bottle Gourd

Preparation time : 30 minutes
Cooking time : 20 minutes

In Bengal, we use a tiny spice called 'radhuni' for this recipe. Radhuni is akin to celery seeds. It has a lovely aroma and taste all its own. Unfortunately, radhuni is not easily available outside Bengal. Do use it if you can procure some: 1 teaspoon, ground to a paste, will do.

INGREDIENTS

Small prawns	~	*250 g*	*Dry red chilli*	~	*1*
Bottle gourd	~	*½ kg*	*Cuminseeds*	~	*1 tsp*
Shelled green peas	~	*½ cup*	*Cumin powder*	~	*1½ tsp*
Turmeric	~	*1 tsp*	*Chilli powder*	~	*1 tsp*
Mustard oil	~	*75 ml*	*Sugar*	~	*1 tbsp*

Radhuni (if available)	~	*1 tsp*	*Garam masala powder*	~	*½ tsp*
			Salt	~	*to taste*

- Shell and devein the prawns. Wash, strain well, smear with a pinch of turmeric and set aside.
- Peel and cut the bottle gourd into tiny cubes, discarding the pith and seeds.
- Pressure cook the gourd with peas for 2 minutes. Do not add water. The gourd will cook in its own juice. Drain.
- Heat oil in a karahi. Temper with dry red chillies and cumin seeds.
- When it pops, add the prawns and stir till they turn pink.
- Add the turmeric, cumin powder, chilli powder, sugar and 'radhuni' paste, if you are using it. Stir fry, sprinkling a little water for a minute.
- Add the cooked gourd and salt. Cook till the water more or less evaporates and you see specks of oil floating.
- Sprinkle garam masala powder and remove.
- Serve with rice.

Macher Kosturi

Fish in Milk

SERVES 4

Preparation time : 30 minutes
Cooking time : 20 minutes

One of the very few fish dishes that do not use turmeric.

INGREDIENTS

Rohu fish	*750 g*	*Chilli powder*	*1 tsp*
Milk	*1 lt*	*Garam masala powder*	*1 tsp*
Ginger	*5 cm piece*	*Refined oil or ghee*	*1/3 cup*
Garlic	*4 cloves*	*Sugar*	*1 tsp*
Onions	*2 large*	***Garnish***	
Salt	*to taste*	*Green chillies*	*6*

- Have the fish cut into 8 pieces.
- Boil the milk till it has reduced by half.

- Grind the ginger, garlic and onion. Strain to extract the juice.
- Marinate the fish in this juice, salt, chilli powder and garam masala powder for 15 minutes.
- Take a large non-stick skillet. Heat oil. Take the skillet off fire and arrange fish pieces without overlapping.
- Return to medium heat. Cook both sides of fish for 2 minutes each. You may have to do it in batches.
- Put all the fish back in the skillet and pour in the thickened milk along with the sugar.
- Reduce the heat once it comes to a boil.
- Cook uncovered till the fish gets done and the gravy is somewhat reduced.
- Serve hot with rice or pulao, garnished with green chillies.

Shorshe Pomfret

Pomfret with Mustard

SERVES 4

Preparation time : 10 minutes
Cooking time : 15 minutes

Any other fish may be used. The process is the same.

INGREDIENTS

Pomfret	~	*½ kg*	*Paanch phoran*	~	*1 tsp*
Turmeric	~	*1 tsp*	*Chilli powder*	~	*1 tsp*
Salt	~	*to taste*	*Green chillies*	~	*4–6*
Mustard oil	~	*75 ml*	*Mustard paste*	~	*1½ tbsp*

- Wash and dry the fish pieces. Smear with a pinch of turmeric and ½ a teaspoon of salt.
- Heat all but 1 tablespoon of oil in a karahi and fry the fish till it turns a light golden colour. You will have to do it in batches. Set aside.

- Heat the oil remaining in the karahi. Temper with paanch phoran.
- When it pops, add the turmeric and chilli powder mixed with a little water.
- Fry till the water dries. Add 1 ½ cups of water, the fish, mustard paste, salt and slit green chillies.
- Cook on high heat till done. There should be a thick gravy.
- Sprinkle the reserved raw mustard oil and remove.

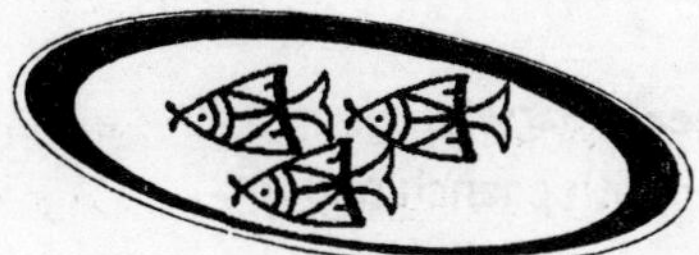

Matarshutir Mach

Fish with Peas

SERVES 4

Preparation time : 15 minutes
Cooking time : 20 minutes

Looks as good as it tastes.

INGREDIENTS

Fish	~	*½ kg*	*Turmeric*	~	*½ tsp*
Green peas	~	*½ kg*	*Chilli powder*	~	*½ tsp*
Mustard oil	~	*4 tbsp*	*Salt*	~	*to taste*
Paanch phoran	~	*1 tsp*	*Green chillies*	~	*4*

- Shell and grind the green peas coarsely.
- Heat oil in a karahi. Temper with paanch phoran.

- When the spices pop, add the ground peas, turmeric, chilli powder and salt. Fry, stirring continually, till the paste darkens and the moisture evaporates. This takes about 10 minutes.
- Add the fish and fry for another 2 minutes. Stir a few times carefully, so as not to break the fish.
- Add a cup of water and the slit green chillies. Cover and cook on reduced heat.
- Remove when the water almost dries up and the fish is cooked.
- This is a moist dish. The peas should cling to fish.

Koi Macher Hara Gouri

SERVES 4

Fish with two kinds of Sauce

Preparation time : 20 minutes
Cooking time : 25 minutes

A rather surprising recipe. The fish tastes sweet sour on one side and pungent on the other. Koi (climbing perch), telapia or even small pomfrets are suitable. Thick fillets or large pieces of rohu and bhetki also work out well.

INGREDIENTS

Fish	~	*8 whole or 8 thick fillets*
Turmeric	~	*1 tsp*
Salt	~	*to taste*
Mustard oil	~	*as required*

Masala No. 1

Turmeric	~	*½ tsp*
Chilli powder	~	*1 tsp*
Mustard paste	~	*2 tbsp*
Salt	~	*to taste*

Green chillies	~	*4*	*Mustard seeds*	~	*a pinch*
Mustard oil	~	*1 tsp*	*Thick tamarind pulp*	~	*4 tbsp*
Paanch phoran	~	*a pinch*	*Sugar*	~	*2 tbsp*
Masala No. 2			*Chilli powder*	~	*1 tsp*
Mustard oil	~	*1 tsp*	*Salt*	~	*to taste*

- Wash and dry the fish. In the case of whole fish, make a few incisions on both sides. Smear with a little salt and turmeric. Set aside.

Masala No. 1

- Mix the turmeric, chilli powder, mustard paste, salt and slit green chillies together.
- Heat oil in a small pan. Temper with paanch phoran. When the spices stop spluttering, add them to the mustard paste. Mix well.

Masala No. 2

- Heat oil. Temper with mustard seeds.
- When they pop, add the tamarind juice, sugar, chilli powder, salt and 1 tablespoon of water. Let it cook.
- Stir continually. Remove when the sauce is of coating consistency.

Finale

- Grease an ovenproof dish large enough to hold the fish comfortably. Or, divide the fish between two dishes.
- Spread masala no. 1 evenly at the bottom. Lay the fish on it. See to it that the masala coats the sides of the fish well.
- Spread a thick coating of masala no. 2 over the fish.
- Preheat the oven to 350°F / 180°C. Bake the fish for 25 minutes.

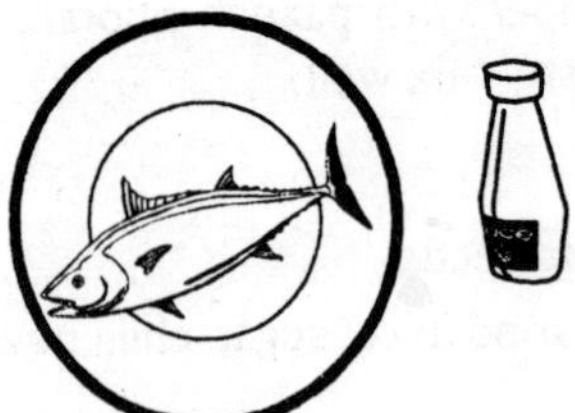

Adar Mach

Fish with Ginger

SERVES 4

Preparation time : 15 minutes
Cooking time : 25 minutes

The advantage of this dish is that even a little goes a long way.

INGREDIENTS

Parwal (Snake gourd)	~	*300 g*	*Sugar*	~	*1 tsp*
Rohu or bhetki	~	*250 g*	*Salt*	~	*to taste*
Turmeric	~	*1 tsp*	*Pure ghee*	~	*2 tsp*
Chilli powder	~	*1 tsp*	*Bay leaves*	~	*2*
Coriander powder	~	*1 tsp*	*Paanch phoran*	~	*1 tsp*
Cumin powder	~	*1 tsp*	*Green chillies*	~	*4*
Mustard paste	~	*2 tsp*	*Ginger paste*	~	*1 tbsp*
Mustard oil	~	*4 tbsp*			

- Peel the parwals. Halve; take out the hard seeds, the tender ones may remain, slice the parwals thinly.
- Boil the fish; discard the bones.
- Mix the turmeric, chilli, coriander, cumin powders and mustard paste with a cup of water. Strain well. Discard the residue. Keep the water.
- Heat oil in a karahi. Put in the parwal and fry till it turns a light brown.
- Add the masala water, sugar and salt. Boil till parwals are cooked and the water is almost absorbed.
- Add the fish. Mix well. The fish gets broken and that is how it should be. Remove and set aside.
- In another pan, heat ghee. Temper with bay leaves, paanch phoran and slit green chillies.
- When they stop spluttering, add the parwal and fish mixture. Stir for a couple of minutes.
- Add the ginger paste. Mix well. Cook for another minute and remove.
- This goes extremely well with plain rice.

Macher Jhuro

Dry Fish Curry

SERVES 4

Preparation time : 15 minutes
Cooking time : 25 minutes

A fish with few bones like surmai or bhetki is preferred or you can use very mature rohu.

INGREDIENTS

Fish	~	*250 g*
Large potatoes	~	*2*
Large onions	~	*2*
Raisins	~	*15*
Mustard oil	~	*1/3 cup*
Bay leaves	~	*2*
Paanch phoran	~	*½ tsp*
Green chillies	~	*4*
Chilli powder	~	*½ tsp*
Turmeric	~	*½ tsp*
Salt	~	*to taste*

- Cut the fish into small pieces.

- Dice the potatoes and onions.
- Soak the raisins.
- Heat half the oil in a karahi. Fry the fish lightly. Keep aside.
- Add the remaining oil to the oil left in the karahi. Temper with bay leaves and paanch phoran.
- When the spices pop, put in the potatoes and onions. Fry well.
- Add the fish, stir.
- Add the raisins, slit green chillies, chilli powder and turmeric. Fry well, sprinkling a little water.
- When a nice aroma emanates, add ¼ cup of water and salt. Cover.
- Cook, stirring often, till the potatotes are done. Never mind if fish get broken. All the ingredients should be well mixed and the water should evaporate.
- This is a very dry fish. It goes well with rotis and parathas.

Macher Kabri

Fish with Milk and Butter

SERVES 6

Preparation time : 5 minutes
Cooking time : 25 minutes

An off-beat recipe; an easy winner in any party.

INGREDIENTS

Fish	~	*1 kg*	*Cinnamon*	~	*5 cm piece*
Refined oil	~	*1 cup*	*Green chillies*	~	*6*
Milk	~	*½ lt*	*Ginger paste*	~	*2 tsp*
Cornflour	~	*1 tbsp*	*Salt*	~	*to taste*
Bay leaves	~	*5*	*Butter*	~	*100 g*
Green cardamom	~	*6*			

Any large white fish will do—like rohu, katla, bhetki. Have the fish cut into medium-sized pieces.

- Heat refined oil in a karahi. Lightly fry the fish and remove.
- Mix cornflour with ¼ cup of milk. Put the rest of the milk on to boil.
- Add the cornflour and cook till milk is reduced by one-fourth.
- Add bay leaves, pounded garam masala, slit green chillies and ginger paste. Cook for a further 5 minutes.
- Add the fish and salt and cook.
- When the fish is done and the gravy is considerably thickened, add the butter. Stir till the butter melts and remove.
- Serve with pulao or ghee bhat.

Macher Tak Jhal

Sour Fish Curry

SERVES 4

Preparation time : 5 minutes
Cooking time : 20 minutes

The Bengalis are the largest fish-eating community. It is not only a staple diet, for many Bengalis it is a passion, a way of life.

INGREDIENTS

Rohu or Surmai fish	~	*½ kg*	*Ginger paste*	~	*1 tsp*
Turmeric	~	*1 tsp*	*Thick curd*	~	*3 tbsp*
Salt	~	*to taste*	*Garam masala powder*	~	*½ tsp*
Mustard oil	~	*¾ cup*	*Amchur*	~	*1 tsp*
Asafoetida	~	*a pinch*	*Green chillies*	~	*2*
Cumin powder	~	*½ tsp*	*Fresh coriander*	~	*2 tbsp*

- Wash the fish; smear with half the turmeric and salt.
- Lightly fry the fish and set aside.
- Remove all but 2 tablespoons of oil in the karahi. Temper with asafoetida.
- When it sizzles, add the cumin powder, ginger paste and turmeric mixed with curd. Fry till it turns brown.
- Add the fish, salt and 1 cup of water.
- Simmer on low heat till done.
- Add garam masala powder, amchur, chopped green chillies and fresh coriander. Cook for another 2 minutes. There should be a semi-thick gravy.

Topse Mach Bhaja

Topse Fish Fry

SERVES 4

Preparation time : 15 minutes
Cooking time : 15 minutes

'Topse' – called mango fish in English – is a very delicate fish, but highly prized for its taste. It is always fried whole.

INGREDIENTS

Topse fish	~	*8*	*Onion juice*	~	*4 tbsp*
Salt	~	*to taste*	*Kalonji*	~	*1 tbsp*
Garlic paste	~	*½ tsp*	*Turmeric*	~	*½ tsp*
Gram flour	~	*200 g*	*Chilli powder*	~	*1 tsp*
Ginger juice	~	*1 tbsp*	*Mustard oil*	~	*1½ cups*

- Clean the fish, keeping them whole. Marinate the fish in salt and garlic paste for 10 minutes.

- Sieve the gram flour and mix with salt, ginger juice, onion juice, kalonji, turmeric and chilli powder.
- Add enough water to make a thick batter.
- Heat oil in a karahi. Dip each fish in the batter; let the extra batter drip off.
- Lower the fish carefully into the hot oil. Fry on medium heat till golden. Fry two fish at a time.
- Serve hot with a chutney or ketchup.
- Any fish or fish fillet can be fried in the same way.

Macher Chorchori

Fish Dry Curry

SERVES 4

Preparation time : 10 minutes + marination

Cooking time : 25 minutes

Use any fish. Small fish like Koi and tangra are particularly good. I use mostly rohu, surmai and bhetki.

INGREDIENTS

Fish	~	*½ kg*
Onions	~	*250 g*
Tomatoes	~	*300 g*
Turmeric	~	*½ tsp*
Chilli powder	~	*1 tsp*
Green chillies	~	*6*
Mustard oil	~	*½ cup*
Salt	~	*to taste*

- Finely chop the onions and tomatoes.
- Mix the fish with all the ingredients, except the oil, and keep it covered for an hour.

- Heat oil in a karahi. Add the fish along with the marinade.
- Stir continually; when it starts to boil, cover and reduce heat.
- Turn the fish over a few times; the fish should be cooked within 10 minutes. Take the fish out and reserve.
- Now, fry the onions and tomatoes. The whole mixture will start looking reddish in colour.
- When the gravy dries and the oil floats on top, add the fish again. Mix carefully and remove.
- It goes well with plain boiled rice.

Chingri Macher Shalmi

SERVES 4

Prawns with Tamarind

Preparation time : 25 minutes
Cooking time : 25 minutes

INGREDIENTS

Tiger prawns	~	*8*	*Garlic*	~	*4 cloves*
Thick tamarind pulp	~	*1½ tbsp*	*Green chillies*	~	*2*
Turmeric	~	*½ tsp*	*Coriander seeds*	~	*1 tsp*
Salt	~	*to taste*	*Dry red chillies*	~	*2*
Large onions	~	*2*	*Sugar*	~	*2 tsp*
Ginger	~	*2 cm piece*	*Mustard oil*	~	*50 g*

- Shell and devein the prawns. Marinate them in a mixture of tamarind, turmeric and salt for 15 minutes.
- Finely chop one onion. Grind the other one along with the ginger, garlic, green chillies, coriander seeds and red chillies.

- Heat oil in a karahi or skillet. Add the chopped onion and fry till light brown.
- Add the ground masala and fry, stirring well, till the oil separates.
- Put in the prawns along with the marinade, sugar and 1 cup of water.
- Cook till the prawns are done and a thick gravy remains. Prawns must never be overcooked; they become tough.
- Serve with rice or a simple pulao.

Vegetables

Shukto (Vegetables with Bitter Gourd)
Mochar Ghonto (Banana Flower Curry)
Aloo Posto (Potatoes with Poppy Seeds)
Paanch Mishuli (Vegetable Medley)
Moricher Jhol (Vegetable Gravy with Pepper)
Pataler Dorma (Stuffed Parwal)
Matarshutir Dhoka (Curried Pea Cubes)

(Continues. . .)

Chanar Korma (Paneer Korma)
Methi Begun (Fenugreek Leaves with Brinjals)
Aam Tel (Mango Pickle)
Kasundi (Mustard–the Bengali Way)
Aamshattor Chatni (Aampapar Chutney)
Peper Plastic Chatni (Raw Papaya Chutney)
Kumror Chokka (Pumpkin Dry Curry)
Enchorer Dum (Raw Jackfruit Curry)

Shukto

Vegetables with Bitter Gourd

SERVES 6

Preparation time : 20 minutes
Cooking time : 25 minutes

If I am asked to name a few typically Bengali dishes, the first one would be 'Shukto', a dish of carefully blended vegetables, in which bitter gourd predominates. This is recipe that Bengali mothers-in-law insist should be a part of every daughter-in-law's repertoire of dishes.

INGREDIENTS

Bottle gourd	~	*1 kg*	*Udad dal varis*	~	*10*
Bitter gourd	~	*1 medium*	*Ginger paste*	~	*1½ tsp*
Mustard seeds	~	*1 tbsp*	*Milk*	~	*1 cup*
Poppy seeds	~	*2 tbsp*	*Sugar*	~	*1 tbsp*
Mustard oil	~	*¼ cup*	*Salt*	~	*to taste*
Paanch phoran	~	*2 tsp*	*Ghee*	~	*1 tbsp*

- Peel, discard the pith and cut the bottle gourd into small cubes and the bitter gourd into rounds.
- Grind mustard seeds and poppy seeds together to a fine paste. Roast and powder half the paanch phoran (i.e., 1 tsp).
- Heat the oil in a karahi, lightly fry the varis and bitter gourd separately and keep aside.
- In the same oil, put in the bottle gourd and ginger paste. Stir fry for 2 minutes.
- Add the milk, sugar, salt, varis, bitter gourd and ½ cup of water. Mix well and cook till the gourd is done. You may pressure cook it for 5 minutes.
- Heat ghee in a karahi. Temper with the whole paanch phoran (i.e., 1 tsp). When it stops spluttering, add the cooked vegetable and boil for 5 minutes.
- Sprinkle the powdered paanch phoran and remove.
- Shukto is always served at room temperature.

Variation: Raw papaya or ripe cucumber may be used the same way.

Mochar Ghonto

SERVES 6

Banana Flower Curry

Preparation time : 30 minutes + soaking
Cooking time : 20 minutes

The cutting of 'mocha' or banana flower is an art. Before you begin, grease your palms with a little oil. Remove the outer petals and take the small bunch of flowers. You will find a transparent petal at the base of each flower and a white match-like stick. Discard them. Now, take a bunch of flowers and cut them into very small pieces. Soak them in water for at least 15 minutes.

INGREDIENTS

Udad dal	~	*100 g*	*Mustard oil*	~	*1 cup*
Peppercorns	~	*5*	*Banana flower, medium*	~	*1*
Coriander seeds	~	*1 tsp*	*Milk*	~	*1 cup*
Cumin seeds	~	*1 tsp*	*Cumin powder*	~	*1 tsp*
Asafoetida	~	*1 pinch*	*Pepper powder*	~	*½ tsp*
Salt	~	*to taste*	*Sugar*	~	*2 tbsp*

Dry red chillies	~	*2*	***Garnish***		
Bay leaves	~	*2*	*Grated coconut*	~	*⅓ cup*

- Soak the udad dal overnight. Grind and mix it with coarsely pounded pepper, coriander, cumin, asafoetida and a pinch of salt. Beat well.
- Heat oil in a karahi. Drop 1 heaped teaspoon of udad dal and fry till golden. Keep these varis aside.
- Cut and soak the banana flower as directed. Strain.
- Boil in fresh water and strain again. You may pressure cook it for 5 minutes.
- Roughly mash the cooked flower. Mix it with milk, cumin powder, pepper powder, sugar and salt.
- Heat 3 tablespoons of oil in a karahi (use the oil left from frying varis). Temper with red chillies and bay leaves.
- Add the banana flower mixture and 1 cup of water. Stir to mix well.
- Cover and cook over medium heat, stirring occasionally.
- When most of the liquid has evaporated and the dish looks moist, remove.
- Garnish with grated coconut and serve.

Aloo Posto

Potatoes with Poppy Seeds

SERVES 6

Preparation time : 10 minutes
Cooking time : 15 minutes

This is a perennial favourite of the Bengalis and is invariably served with udad dal. Each family has its own particular version. If you soak the poppy seeds for an hour, you'll find the grinding easier.

INGREDIENTS

Potatoes	~	*½ kg*	*Paanch phoran*	~	*1 tsp*
Poppy seeds	~	*100 g*	*Salt*	~	*to taste*
Green chillies	~	*8*	*Turmeric*	~	*1 tsp*
Mustard oil	~	*100 ml*			

- Peel and cut the potatoes into small cubes.

- Roast 2 teaspoons of poppy seeds in a karahi till a shade darker. Set aside. Grind the rest with 2 green chillies.
- Heat three-fourths of the oil in the same karahi. Season with the paanch phoran.
- When they stop crackling, add the potatoes and fry till it turns a light golden colour.
- Add 1 cup of water, salt, green chillies and turmeric and cover.
- Cook over a moderate heat. When the potatoes are cooked, add the poppy-seed paste and the remaining oil. Stir till everything gets mixed and moisture dries up.
- Remove from heat and sprinkle the roasted poppy seeds.

Note: Virtually any vegetable can be cooked the same way—ladies' fingers, parwal (snake gourd) and ridge gourd taste particularly good.

Paanch Mishuli

Vegetable Medley

SERVES 6

Preparation time : 15 minutes
Cooking time : 25 minutes

The choice of vegetables depends on the season.

INGREDIENTS

Potatoes	~	*250 g*	*Paanch phoran*	~	*2 tsp*
Pumpkin	~	*250 g*	*Green chillies*	~	*6*
Brinjal	~	*250 g*	*Ginger paste*	~	*2 tsp*
Parwals (Snake gourd)	~	*200 g*	*Mustard oil*	~	*1/3 cup*
Broad beans	~	*100 g*	*Turmeric*	~	*1 tsp*
Ridge gourd	~	*200 g*	*Sugar*	~	*1 tbsp*
Shelled peas	~	*½ cup*	*Salt*	~	*to taste*

- Peel the potatoes, pumpkin and ridge gourd. Pare the parwals at intervals. Cut all the vegetables uniformly into small cubes.
- Heat oil in a karahi till it starts to smoke. Temper with paanch phoran. When they splutter, add ginger paste, and stir once.
- Put in the hard vegetables first—that is, potatoes and parwal. After a couple of minutes, add the other vegetables and salt.
- Stir fry for 5 minutes.
- Add the turmeric, sugar, salt and slit green chillies. Stir to mix well. Cover.
- The vegetables will give out a lot of water. So do not add extra water. Uncover when vegetables are three-fourths done.
- Let the moisture evaporate almost completely. This should be a wet curry.
- It goes well with rice, chapattis or puris.
- During the season, you can use cauliflower, French beans and carrots.

Moricher Jhol

Vegetable Gravy with Pepper

SERVES 4

Preparation time : 15 minutes
Cooking time : 25 minutes

INGREDIENTS

Potatoes, medium	~	*2*	*Nigella*	~	*½ tsp*
Long brinjals	~	*2*	*Dry red chillies*	~	*2*
Parwals (Snake gourd)	~	*4*	*Salt*	~	*to taste*
Flour	~	*1 tsp*	*Sugar*	~	*1 tsp*
Ridge gourd, large	~	*1*	*Pepper powder*	~	*1 tbsp*
Drumsticks	~	*4*	*Grated coconut*	~	*2 tbsp*
Mustard oil	~	*4 tbsp*	*Coriander leaves*	~	*a handful*
*Udad dal varis**	~	*10–12*			

- Peel all the vegetables (except brinjals) and cut into long finger-like pieces.
- Heat oil in a karahi. Fry the varis and remove.

- Temper the same oil with nigella and dry chillies.
- Add the vegetables, salt and sugar. Stir fry till the moisture dries up a little for about 4 minutes.
- Add 3 cups of water and cook covered on medium heat.
- When the vegetables are three-fourths done, add the grated coconut, fried varis, slit green chillies and freshly ground pepper.
- Mix 1 teaspoon of flour with ¼ cup of gravy and add to the vegetables.
- Cook till the vegetables are done. Add coriander leaves and remove.

Variation: Other seasonal vegetables may be used.

* *Varis are dried udad dal paste. These are easily available in the market.*

Pataler Dorma

Stuffed Parwal

SERVES 6

Preparation time : 30 minutes
Cooking time : 20 minutes

INGREDIENTS

Parwals (Snake gourd)	~	*12*	*Green chillies*	~	*2*
Mustard oil	~	*1 cup*	*Sugar*	~	*½ tsp*
For the Stuffing:			*Salt*	~	*¼ tsp*
Grated coconut	~	*¾ cup*	*Raisins*	~	*12*
Grated khoya	~	*½ cup*	*Chopped cashewnuts*	~	*2 tbsp*
Grated ginger	~	*1 tsp*			

- Mix all the ingredients for the stuffing together. Keep aside.
- Wash and peel the parwals at intervals.
- Make a slit in the middle of each parwal keeping the stem ends intact.

- With a clean hairpin or the back of a spoon, take out the pith and seeds and discard.
- Divide the stuffing into 12 portions and stuff one portion into each parwal. Do not stuff too tightly, leave a little space. The filling will expand during frying.
- Secure the opening of the parwals with thread.
- Heat oil in a karahi. Fry parwals in two batches, till done. Serve hot.
- Any other stuffing, like keema, prawns, fish or paneer may be used. You may even prepare a gravy and pour it over the fried parwals.

Anytime Salad!

If you run out of green vegetables for salad, mix some finely chopped onions with boiled chickpeas (kabuli chana) and serve.

Matarshutir Dhoka

Curried Pea Cubes

SERVES 4

Preparation time : 30 minutes
Cooking time : 25 minutes

INGREDIENTS

For the Dhoka:

Shelled green peas	~	*2 cups*
Ginger paste	~	*1½ tsp*
Aniseed paste	~	*1 tsp*
Chilli powder	~	*½ tsp*
Gram flour	~	*2 tbsp*
Sugar	~	*½ tsp*
Salt	~	*½ tsp*
Mustard oil	~	*1 cup*

For the curry:

Mustard oil	~	*3 tbsp*
Cumin seeds	~	*1 tsp*
Pure ghee	~	*1 tbsp*
Potatoes	~	*200 g*
Turmeric	~	*½ tsp*
Chilli powder	~	*1 tsp*
Curd	~	*1/3 cup*
Ginger paste	~	*1 tsp*
Sugar	~	*½ tsp*
Garam masala powder	~	*½ tsp*
Asafoetida	~	*a pinch*
Salt	~	*to taste*

For the Dhokas:

- Grind the peas.
- Heat 3 tablespoons of oil in a karahi. Add the peas and the rest of the ingredients.
- Stir to mix well. Fry till the mixture starts to leave the sides of the karahi.
- Grease a thali. Spread the pea mixture on it evenly, to a thickness of about 1½ cm.
- When cool, cut into square pieces.
- Heat oil in a karahi. Deep fry the pea squares till brown. Keep aside.

For the curry:

- Heat the oil and ghee together in a karahi. Temper with whole cumin seeds.
- Put in the diced potatoes and fry for 2–3 minute.
- Add all the other ingredients except asafoetida and garam masala.
- Fry for 5 minutes. Add sufficient water. The 'dhokas' will soak up a lot of gravy. Cover and cook till the potatoes are done.
- Uncover and add the 'dhokas'. Let it boil for a couple of minutes.
- Mix asafoetida in ¼ cup of water. Add to the curry along with the garam masala powder.
- Cook for another two minutes and remove.

Chanar Korma

Paneer Korma

SERVES 4

Preparation time : 20 minutes
Cooking time : 20 minutes

INGREDIENTS

Paneer	~	*300 g*	*Salt*	~	*to taste*
Refined oil	~	*½ cup*	*Sugar*	~	*1 tbsp*
Cashewnuts	~	*50 g*	*Curd*	~	*2 tbsp*
Raisins	~	*50 g*	*Cumin powder*	~	*1 tsp*
Tomatoes	~	*2*	*Coriander powder*	~	*1 tsp*
Onions	~	*2*	*Pepper powder*	~	*1 tsp*
Ginger	~	*2½ cm piece*	*Mace powder*	~	*½ tsp*
Green chillies	~	*4*	*Nutmeg powder*	~	*½ tsp*
Turmeric	~	*1/3 tsp*			

- Dice the paneer. Lightly fry it and keep it soaked in warm water. This will keep the paneer soft.

- Fry the cashewnuts and raisins in the same oil. Set aside.
- Finely chop the onions and tomatoes. Grate the ginger. Beat the curd.
- In a karahi, heat the oil left over after frying paneer. Fry the onions till they turn pink.
- Add the ginger, tomatoes and slit green chillies. Stir till the tomatoes turn soft.
- Add turmeric, salt, sugar, cumin, coriander and pepper powders.
- Fry for 2–3 minutes, stirring all the while.
- Add 1 cup of water, paneer, cashewnuts and raisins. Stir to mix well.
- Cover, reduce the flame and boil for 5–7 minutes.
- Uncover, sprinkle mace powder and grated nutmeg, and remove.

Methi Begun

Fenugreek Leaves with Brinjals

SERVES 4

Preparation time : 15 minutes
Cooking time : 15 minutes

INGREDIENTS

Brinjals	~	*250 g*	*Mustard paste*	~	*1 tbsp*
Fresh fenugreek leaves bunch	~	*1 large*	*Salt*	~	*to taste*
Mustard oil	~	*1/3 cup*	*Ginger paste*	~	*2 tsp*

- Pick and wash the fenugreek leaves. Chop the brinjals into small cubes.
- Heat half the oil in a karahi. Add the brinjals, stir fry till done. Remove.
- Heat the remaining oil in the same karahi. Add the fenugreek leaves and stir fry till the moisture given out dries up. Fry for another minute.
- Add the fried brinjal, mustard paste, salt and ginger paste.
- Mix, stirring well. Cook for 2 minutes.
- Remove and serve with rice.

Aam Tel

Mango Pickle

Yield	:	1½ kg
Preparation time	:	2 days
Maturing	:	2–3 weeks

Bengal does not boast of a vast repertoire of pickles, unlike other states like say, Gujarat or Tamil Nadu. But the few that there are, have a most distinctive taste. The following recipe is my grandmother's speciality given to me by my mother.

INGREDIENTS

Green mangoes	~	*1½ kg*	*Turmeric*	~	*2 tbsp*
Salt	~	*3 tbsp*	*Chilli powder*	~	*1½ tbsp*
Paanch phoran	~	*5 tbsp*	*Asafoetida*	~	*2 tbsp*
Whole dry red chillies	~	*20*	*Mustard oil*	~	*500 ml*
Mustard seeds	~	*6 tbsp*			

- Wash the mangoes and wipe them until they are absolutely dry. Cut the mangoes into 8 long pieces each; discard the stones.
- Grind mustard seeds to a coarse powder.
- Smear the mango pieces with salt, paanch phoran and dry chillies. Keep in the sun for a day. The mangoes will give out a lot of water.
- Put the mango pieces in dry jars along with the rest of the ingredients and the accumulated water.
- Top with mustard oil. The mangoes must be immersed in oil. If necessary, add more oil.
- Keep it in the sun for at least 15 days.
- The pickle will be ready to eat within 3 weeks. It keeps indefinitely and matures with age.

Relish Your Pickles

If your pickle jar seems to be getting a fungus layer on top, coat the outside of the jar with salt and mustard oil.

Kasundi

Mustard—the Bengali Way

Makes : 1 large bottle
Preparation time : A few days

A Bengali version of mustard, it is widely used in Bengali cuisine. It can also be served as a dip.

INGREDIENTS

Brown mustard seeds	~	*500 g*	*Bay leaves*	~	*4*
Ginger	~	*25 g*	*Dry red chillies*	~	*5*
Whole piece of turmeric	~	*10 g*	*Salt*	~	*to taste*

- Pick and wash the mustard seeds. Drain well. Dry on a piece of cloth.
- Finely shred the ginger. Wash all the ingredients except the salt.
- Dry all these in the sun for 3–4 days.

- Dry grind them finely. Sieve and grind the residue once more. The resulting powder should be very fine.
- Boil 2 litres of water for 15 minutes.
- Take half the water and add the powdered masala and salt to taste. Stir well to mix and allow it to come to a boil. Remove immediately.
- The consistency should be thinner than tomato ketchup. If it is too thick, add more hot water.
- Pour into sterilised bottles.
- Keep the bottle in the sun for 10–15 days and then use.
- It keeps well for a few months.

Amshattor Chatni

Sweet Aampapar Chutney

SERVES 8–10

Preparation time : 5 minutes
Cooking time : 25 minutes

One can buy sweet aampapar in Bengal. They are used in various ways, as filling for sandesh, in kheer and above all, in this wonderful chutney. They are delicious, eaten by themselves, too.

INGREDIENTS

Sweet aampapar	~	*1 pkt*
Dates	~	*100 g*
Sugar	~	*½ cup*
Raisins	~	*50 g*
Limes	~	*4*
Roasted and powdered paanch phoran	~	*1 tsp*

- Cut the aampapar into small cubes. Deseed and cut each date into 4 pieces.
- Put sugar and 1½ cups of water to boil.

- Once it starts to boil, add the dates and raisins and cook till the syrup is reduced by one fourth.
- Add the aampapar and cook till thick, stirring all the while. The aampapar will disintegrated and thicken the chutney.
- Add lime juice. Sprinkle the roasted and powdered paanch phoran and remove.
- Serve chilled.

Variation: Tomatoes and pineapple may be added, too.

Chilli-Ginger Pickle

Chop green chillies and ginger into small pieces and store them in a bottle of salted lime juice. Refrigerate for a few days. The pickle will keep for a long time.

Peper Plastic Chatni

SERVES 8

Raw Papaya Chutney

Preparation time : 30 minutes +
1 hour for soaking
Cooking time : 25 minutes

This dish gets this quaint name thanks to the papaya bits that do look like small transparent plastic pieces. I have seen in my mother painstakingly cutting the raw papayas into fine square pieces, almost see-through. With time and patience, both being at a premium nowadays, I prefer to grate the papaya.

INGREDIENTS

Green papaya	~	*1 kg*	*Salt*	~	*a pinch*
Edible lime	~	*½ tsp*	*Limes*	~	*3*
Sugar	~	*250 g*	*Glace cherries, chopped*	~	*1 tbsp*
Grated ginger	~	*1 tsp*			

- Wash, peel, discard the seeds and grate the papaya. Soak it in water, adding the edible lime (the kind used in 'paan') for about an hour. Wash thoroughly and drain well.
- Pressure cook the papaya without water for a couple of minutes. Strain.
- Add ½ a cup of water to the sugar and heat. Stir till the sugar dissolves. Boil till the syrup thickens a little.
- Add the ginger, papaya and salt. Let them cook till very little water is left.
- Remove from the heat and add lime juice.
- Garnish with chopped glade cherries. Cool and serve.

Instant Chutney

Mix 1 tsp mango powder (amchur) with ¼ tsp cumin (jeera) powder, 3 tsp sugar, ½ cup water and boil for 2-5 minutes on low heat.

Kumror Chokka

SERVES 4

Pumpkin Dry Curry

Preparation time : 10 minutes
Cooking time : 20 minutes

INGREDIENTS

Chick peas	~	*¼ cup*	*Chilli powder*	~	*1 tsp*
Pumpkin	~	*½ kg*	*Cumin powder*	~	*1 tsp*
Mustard oil	~	*2 tbsp*	*Turmeric*	~	*½ tsp*
Paanch phoran	~	*1 tsp*	*Salt*	~	*to taste*
Bay leaves	~	*2*	*Sugar*	~	*1 tsp*
Dry red chillies	~	*2*	*Pure ghee*	~	*1 tbsp*
Ginger paste	~	*1 tsp*	*Garam masala powder*	~	*1 tsp*

- Soak the chick peas overnight; cut the pumpkin into cubes.
- Heat oil in a karahi. Temper with paanch phoran, bay leaves and red chillies. Put in them pumpkin pieces and fry well for 5 minutes.

- Add the chick peas, all the spices, sugar and salt, except the garam masala. Fry for 2–3 minutes.
- Add ¾ cup of water and cover. Reduce the heat and cook till done. There should not be any extra gravy. Boil till excess liquid, if any, evaporates.
- Sprinkle the garam masala powder and pure ghee.
- Mix well. This is a rather wet dish. The pumpkins may break while stirring, but that's okay.

Atta to the Rescue

If you feel you have over-salted a dish, put it to boil and while it is cooking, add a small ball of rice flour or wholewheat flour (atta). This will absorb the extra salt.

Enchorer Dum

Raw Jackfruit Curry

SERVES 4

Preparation time : 20 minutes
Cooking time : 35 minutes

INGREDIENTS

Raw jackfruit	~	*500 g*
Chopped onion	~	*1 cup*
Mustard oil	~	*6 tbsp*
Asafoetida	~	*1 pinch*
Bay leaves	~	*2*
Green cardamoms	~	*4*
Cloves	~	*4*
Cinnamon	~	*5 cm stick*
Turmeric	~	*1 tsp*
Chilli powder	~	*1 tsp*
Curd	~	*½ cup*
Salt	~	*to taste*
Sugar	~	*2 tsp*
Raisins	~	*15–20*
Ghee	~	*1 tbsp*
Green chillies	~	*2*
Ginger paste	~	*1 tbsp*
Coconut paste	~	*1 tbsp*

- Peel and cut the jackfruit into large cubes.

- Parboil the jackfruit pieces in pressure cooker with 1½ cups of water for 5 minutes. Release pressure and drain.
- Heat oil in a karahi till it smokes. Temper with asafoetida, bay leaves, green cardamoms, cloves and cinnamon.
- When they change colour, add the onions and fry till golden in colour.
- Add the turmeric, chilli powder, ginger paste and coconut paste mixed with 1/8 cup of water. Stir till the moisture evaporates.
- Add the beaten curd and fry for 2 minutes or till the oil surfaces.
- Add the jackfruit pieces, salt, sugar and raisins and fry for another couple of minutes.
- Add 2 cups of hot water and cook covered for 5 minutes, stirring it 2–3 times in between.
- Reduce the heat and cook for another 15 minutes, stirring a few times.
- Add the ghee and slit green chillies. Remove and keep covered till needed.

Useful Substitute

Crushed cornflakes are a useful substitute for dried breadcrumbs for coating food before frying. Use them in stuffing too, in place of breadcrumbs.

Meat /Chicken Dishes

Kasha Mangsho (Dry Meat Curry)
Robibarer Mangsho (Sunday Meat Curry)
Panthar Bangla (Meat Curry–Bengali Way)
Mete Chorchori (Liver Curry)

Kasha Mangsho

Dry Meat Curry

SERVES 6

Preparation time : 20 minutes
Cooking time : 1–1½ hour

The success of this recipe depends on freshly-ground spices. Readymade spice powders are taboo!

INGREDIENTS

Meat	~	*1 kg*	*Peppercorns*	~	*10*
Dry red chillies	~	*6*	*Onion*	~	*250 g*
Ginger	~	*50 g*	*Mustard oil*	~	*175 ml*
Garlic	~	*1 whole pod*	*Turmeric*	~	*1 tsp*
Coriander seeds	~	*1½ tbsp*	*Salt*	~	*to taste*
Cumin seeds	~	*1½ tsp*	*Bay leaves*	~	*4*

The meat should be tender and cut into small pieces.

- Grind the ginger, garlic and chillies together.
- Roast the coriander, cumin and peppercorns lightly, and grind to a powder.
- Cut the onions into thin circles.
- Heat oil in a degchi till it starts smoking. Add the onion rings. Fry till they turn a light brown.
- Add the ground paste, turmeric, salt and bay leaves, and fry for a couple of minutes.
- Add the meat and fry, stirring continually till the moisture released by the meat dries up.
- Add enough hot water to cover and let it cook. Sorry, no pressure cooking!
- Fry well once the meat is done, till all the moisture evaporates.
- Sprinkle the powdered spices. Mix well. This has no gravy, save what is clinging to the meat.
- Serve hot with chapattis or parathas.

Note: You may use chicken also.

Robibarer Mangsho

Sunday Meat Curry

SERVES 4

Preparation time : 15 minutes + marination

Cooking time : 1–1 ½ hours

Bengalis, in general, are great carnivores. For some strange reason, it's become almost a ritual in most Bengali households to have meat for lunch on Sundays. Come Sunday, and you'll find a long queue outside meat shops. Even our family in Delhi, where I grew up, was no exception. This is my mother's speciality.

INGREDIENTS

Onions, large	~	*6*	*Turmeric*	~	*¾ tsp*
Tomatoes, large	~	*2*	*Sugar*	~	*2 tsp*
Potatoes, medium	~	*6*	*Ginger paste*	~	*1 tbsp*
Meat	~	*½ kg*	*Garlic paste*	~	*1 tsp*
Salt	~	*to taste*	*Coriander powder*	~	*½ tbsp*

Cumin powder	~	*½ tbsp*	*Mustard oil*	~	*½ cup*
Pepper powder	~	*1 tsp*	*Ghee*	~	*1 tbsp*
Chilli powder	~	*1 tsp*	*Garam masala powder*	~	*½ tsp*
Bay leaves	~	*2*			

- Chop the onions; cut the tomatoes into quarters. Peel and halve the potatoes.
- Wash the meat and marinate in all the ingredients except ghee and add 1 tablespoon of oil. Marinate for as long as time permits, the minimum being one hour.
- Heat remaining oil in a degchi. Add the meat along with the marinade. Stir and cover well.
- The meat will give out some water. Cook, stirring occasionally, till the water dries up.
- Add hot water to cook the meat. Cover.
- When the meat is parboiled, add the potatoes. Cook till both the meat and potatoes are well done.
- Heat ghee in a small frying pan. Season with garam masala powder.
- Add to the meat. Cook for another couple of minutes. There should be a semi-thick gravy.
- This can also be pressure cooked for 15 minutes. Add the potatoes along with the water in that case.

Note: Chicken may be cooked in the same way.

Panthar Bangla

Meat Curry—Bengali Way

SERVES 6

Preparation time : 10 minutes
Cooking time : 40 minutes

Somehow, in spite of being great meat eaters, meat cookery has never been our forte. Elaborate meat preparations are latter-day innovations influenced by Mughlai cooking or Western cuisine. This is a simple but very tasty meat curry generally cooked in Bengali households.

INGREDIENTS

Meat	~	*1 kg*	*Mustard oil*	~	*3 tbsp*
Potatoes	~	*300 g*	*Bay leaves*	~	*1½ tsp*
Onions, medium	~	*2*	*Ginger paste*	~	*2*
Onions, large	~	*3*	*Turmeric*	~	*1 tsp*
Ghee	~	*1 tbsp*	*Chilli powder*	~	*1 tsp*

Coriander powder	~	*1 tbsp*	*Salt*	~	*to taste*
Curd	~	*250 g*	*Roasted and powdered cumin*	~	*2 tsp*
Sugar	~	*1 tsp*			

- Cut the mutton into medium pieces.
- Peel and cube the potatoes.
- Heat oil and ghee together in a degchi. Temper with bay leaves.
- Add the ground large onions, ginger paste, turmeric, chilli and coriander powders and beaten curd. Stir to mix well.
- Fry, stirring continually, for 10 minutes.
- Add sugar, salt, meat and medium-sized onions, diced. Stir fry for another 5 minutes.
- Add 6 cups of hot water and cover. When it comes to a boil, reduce the heat to medium.
- After about 15 minutes of cooking time, add the potatoes. Cook till the meat is done.
- There should be a medium-thick gravy. Sprinkle the roasted and powdered cumin and remove.
- Serve with rice.

Mete Chorchori

Liver Curry

SERVES 4

Preparation time : 15 minutes
Cooking time : 25 minutes

INGREDIENTS

Potatoes, medium	~	*2*	*Paanch phoran*	~	*1 tsp*
Liver	~	*250 g*	*Green chillies*	~	*2*
Onions	~	*2*	*Salt*	~	*to taste*
Tomatoes	~	*2*	*Turmeric*	~	*¼ tsp*
Mustard oil	~	*3 tbsp*			

- Peel and cut the potatoes into juliennes. Cut the liver into thin pieces. Chop the onions and tomatoes.
- Heat oil in a karahi. Add paanch phoran.
- As soon as they splutter, add the potatoes, slit green chillies, salt and turmeric. Fry for another two minutes.

- Sprinkle half-a-cup of water. Cover and reduce the heat.
- After 5 minutes, add the liver pieces. Stir well. Cover.
- Uncover after 10 minutes. Both the potatoes and liver should be done by now. Stir and let the excess liquid evaporate.
- There should be no gravy.
- Serve with puris or chapattis.

Oil (less) Food!

If you're health conscious and worried about extra oil in your food, don't worry! After cooking a dish, refrigerate it and remove the solidified fat before reheating it.

Snacks

Matarshutir Kochuri (Green Pea Kachauri)
Radhabollobhi (Udad Dal Puries)
Hinger Kochuri (Kachauri with Asafoetida)
Chingri Cutlet (Prawn Cutlet)
Panthar Ghugni (Chick Peas with Minced Meat)
Phulko Luchi (Bengali Puri)
Kabiraji Katlet (Minced Meat Cutlet)
Nimki (Fried Flour Bits)
Mochar Chop (Banana Flower Kababs)

Matarshutir Kochuri

MAKES 12

Green Pea Kachauri

Preparation time : 1 hour
Cooking time : 30 minutes

Though called kachauri, these are actually puris stuffed with green peas. They go very well with 'aloor dum'.

INGREDIENTS

For the stuffing:

Green peas ~ *600 g*
Ginger ~ *2½ cm piece*
Asafoetida ~ *a generous pinch*
Fennel seeds ~ *1½ tsp*
Refined oil ~ *2 tbsp*
Whole cumin seed ~ *½ tsp*
Chilli powder ~ *½ tsp*
Sugar ~ *2 tsp*
Salt ~ *to taste*

For the covering:

Flour ~ *250 g*
Baking powder ~ *a pinch*
Salt ~ *½ tsp*
Ghee or refined oil ~ *3 tbsp*
Refined oil ~ *for deep frying*

- Shell and grind the peas along with ginger and asafoetida. Grind the fennel seeds separately.
- Heat oil in a karahi—a non-stick one helps. Add the cumin seeds.
- When they stop spluttering, add the ground peas. Fry, stirring continually.
- Add the fennel-seed paste, chilli powder, sugar and salt. Keep stirring till the mixture becomes a dark green in colour and leaves the sides of the pan.
- Remove and cool.

For the covering:

- Sieve flour with baking powder and salt, rub in ghee or oil and make a dough with water as needed, knead well; the dough should be soft and pliable.
- Divide it into 12 portions. Take one portion and roll into a thick round.
- Divide the stuffing into 12 parts and put one part in the centre of each flour round. Pleat the sides and bring to the centre and shape into a ball again.
- Roll into a puri with the help of a little oil. Take care that the stuffing does not come out.
- Heat enough oil in a karahi for deep frying.
- Deep fry the kachauris, one at a time. They should puff up and be a light brown in colour.
- Serve hot.

Radhabollobhi

Udad Dal Puries

MAKES 18–20

Preparation time : 40 minutes + soaking
Cooking time : 30 minutes

You can use only water for kneading the dough. But my mother always uses milk and that's what I use too.

INGREDIENTS

For the pastry:

Flour	~	*500 g*
Salt	~	*1 tsp*
Oil or ghee	~	*3 tbsp*
Milk	~	*2 cups*
Refined oil	~	*for deep frying*

For the filling:

Udad dal	~	*200 g*
Coriander seeds	~	*2 tsp*
Cumin seeds	~	*2 tsp*
Dry red chillies	~	*4*
Peppercorns	~	*5*
Salt	~	*1 tsp*
Refined oil	~	*2 tbsp*

For the pastry:

- Sieve the flour and salt together.
- Add oil or ghee and mix till the mixture resembles breadcrumbs.
- Add milk and knead to a dough. If necessary, add water. Knead very well till the dough is soft and elastic.
- Divide it into 18–20 parts.
- Roll each part into a ball and then pat it with the hands to a large disc.
- Stuff with 1 portion of the filling and roll into a ball again.
- Roll out into a slightly thick puri with the help of a little oil, taking care that the filling does not come out.
- Heat enough oil for deep frying in a karahi. Fry one puri at a time till light golden.
- Serve hot with a vegetable curry.

For the filling:

- Soak the dal overnight. Grind to a fine paste.
- Roast lightly and powder coriander, cumin seeds, dry chillies and peppercorns.
- Add the salt and powdered spices to the dal paste and mix well.
- Heat oil in a karahi. Add the dal paste and fry well for 8–10 minutes on medium heat.
- Remove, divide into 18–20 portions, and use as directed.

Hinger Kochuri

Kachauri with Asafoetida

MAKES 8–10

Preparation time : 30 minutes + overnight soaking

Cooking time : 30 minutes

In Bengal, we use what is known as 'matar dal' along with gram dal. Do use it if you can get hold of some. Otherwise, udad dal is a good substitute.

INGREDIENTS

For the pastry:

Flour	~	*250 g*
Salt	~	*½ tsp*
Refined oil or ghee	~	*1½ tbsp*
Refined oil	~	*for deep frying*

For the filling:

Bengal gram dal	~	*100 g*
Udad dal	~	*50 g*
Ginger paste	~	*2½ tsp*
Fennel seed paste	~	*2½ tsp*

Chilli powder	~	*2½ tsp*	*Salt*	~	*to taste*
Asafoetida	~	*¼ tsp*	*Refined oil*	~	*1½ tbsp*

For the pastry:

- Sieve the flour and salt together. Rub with ghee or oil till the mixture resembles breadcrumbs.
- Knead with water to a smooth and elastic dough.
- Divide it into 8–10 parts. Fill each part with one portion of the filling and roll out into a puri with the help of a little oil.
- Heat enough oil in a karahi for deep frying.
- Fry one puri at a time till a light brown.
- Serve hot with a dal.

For the filling:

- Soak both the dals overnight. Drain and grind to a paste.
- Heat the oil in a karahi. Add the dal paste along with all the other ingredients.
- Fry, stirring well for 7–8 minutes.
- Divide into 8–10 parts and use as directed.

Chingri Cutlet

Prawn Cutlet

SERVES 6

Preparation time : 20 minutes + marination

Cooking time : 20 minutes

A most satisfying snack.

INGREDIENT

Tiger prawns	~	*6*	*Salt*	~	*to taste*
Onion juice	~	*2 tbsp*	*Egg*	~	*1*
Garlic juice	~	*1 tbsp*	*Dry breadcrumbs*	~	*1 cup*
Vinegar	~	*¼ cup*	*Refined oil*	~	*1 cup*

- Shell the prawns, leaving the tail tips on. Devein, and discard the heads.
- Slit the prawns lengthwise, but do not cut through. Flatten the prawns slightly with the back of a knife.

- Marinate prawns in onion-garlic juice, vinegar and salt for an hour or even longer, if time permits.
- Take out the prawns from the marinade, dip in the beaten egg and coat uniformly with bread crumbs.
- Let prawns remain thus for 15 minutes.
- Heat oil in a karahi. Shake off the excess crumbs from the prawns; fry two at a time till golden-brown.
- Serve immediately with a chutney and a salad.

Panthar Ghugni

Chick Peas with Minced Meat

SERVES 6

Preparation time : 25 minutes + soaking
Cooking time : 30 minutes

A classic dish of Bengal. It is invariably made during 'Bijoya dashami',–the last day of Durga puja. The vegetarian version uses coconut.

INGREDIENTS

White chick peas	~	*250 g*	*Chilli powder*	~	*1 tsp*
Onion, large	~	*1*	*Cumin powder*	~	*1 tsp*
Potato, large	~	*1*	*Coriander powder*	~	*1 tsp*
Salt	~	*to taste*	*Curd*	~	*2½ tbsp*
Turmeric	~	*1 tsp*	*Minced meat*	~	*250 g*
Mustard oil	~	*4 tbsp*	*Green chillies*	~	*2*
Ginger, grated	~	*1 tbsp*	*Garam masala powder*	~	*½ tsp*

- Soak the chick peas overnight.
- Finely slice the onions. Peel and dice the potatoes.
- Boil the chick peas in a pressure cooker with potatoes, 1 teaspoon of salt and ½ a teaspoon of turmeric for 20 minutes. You may add a pinch of soda to make the peas more tender.
- Heat oil in a karahi. Fry the onions till they turn a light brown.
- Add all the ingredients except the green chillies, garam masala and salt.
- Fry well. When the oil separates, add salt and 1 cup of water. Cover.
- Remove when the mince is done and the excess liquid, if any, has evaporated.
- Mix the cooked mince and chick peas together. Put on a high flame.
- Add the chopped green chillies. Cook well, stirring, till very little gravy remains.
- Add the garam masala powder and remove.

Phulko Luchi

Bengali Puri

MAKES 18–20

Preparation time : 20 minutes
Cooking time : 15 minutes

The difference between the 'luchi' of Bengal and the puri of North India is that the former is invariably made with refined flour and is thinner; while the 'puri' is made of wholewheat flour and is thicker.

INGREDIENTS

Refined flour	~	*250 g*	*Salt*	~	*½ tsp*
Ghee or oil	~	*2 tbsp*	*Ghee or refined oil*	~	*as needed*

- Sieve the flour and salt into a bowl. Rub in 2 tablespoons of ghee or oil.
- Add water gradually and knead into a soft and smooth dough. Divide it into 18–20 balls.
- Lightly grease a rolling board and pin. Roll each ball out into a thin puri. You'll have to grease the board a few times in between.
- Heat ghee or oil in a karahi till it starts smoking. Drop in one 'luchi' at a time. Press gently with a flat, perforated spoon.
- The luchi will puff up. Turn it over and fry the other side. The whole procedure will not take even a minute. Hold the luchi for a few seconds against the side of the karahi to let extra oil drain. Remove.
- The luchis must remain white. Regulate the heat as needed. Serve immediately.

Colour Fast

Green chillies kept in an airtight bottle with a pinch of turmeric powder and placed on a window sill, will retain their colour.

Kabiraji Katlet

Minced Meat Cutlet

SERVES 6

Preparation time : 10 minutes + marination
Cooking time : 30 minutes

The influence of the British Raj is clearly seen in this recipe. The art of breading and frying was brought in by the British and the French. This is of course, a spicier version of the British cutlet.

INGREDIENTS

Minced meat	~	*½ kg*
Very finely-chopped onions	~	*2*
Ginger paste	~	*1 tsp*
Garlic paste	~	*½ tsp*
Green chillies	~	*3*
Gram flour or rice flour	~	*1 tbsp*
Curd	~	*1 tbsp*
Pepper powder	~	*1 tsp*
Chilli powder roasted and powdered Cumin seeds	~	*½ tsp*
Garam masala powder	~	*½ tsp*
Coriander leaves	~	*½ cup*
Lime	~	*1*
Eggs	~	*3*

Dry breadcrumbs	~	*as needed*	*Refined oil*	~	*for frying*
Salt	~	*to taste*			

- Mix the minced meat with all the ingredients except the eggs, breadcrumbs and oil. Also add lime juice. Keep it aside for an hour.
- Mix once more using your hands. The mixture will now be somewhat soft. Mix ¼ cup of breadcrumbs or as needed and knead to make a dough.
- Divide the mince into 12 portions. Form each portion into a ball, then flatten into a square shape, almost a centimetre thick.
- Beat one egg with 1 tablespoon of water.
- Dip each cutlet into the beaten egg, then coat with dry breadcrumbs.
- Deep fry the cutlets in hot oil in a karahi till a light brown and keep aside.
- Beat the other 2 eggs with a tablespoon of water and a pinch of salt till frothy.

For the Garnish:

- Heat the oil once more on medium heat. Dip your fingers in the beaten egg and let the egg drip into the oil from your fingers.
- The egg drops will at once curl up and form a lacy pattern. Do not let them brown. Take them out at once with a slotted spoon.
- Fry all the egg this way and garnish the cutlets with it.

Nimki

Fried Flour Bits

MAKES 10

Preparation time : 30 minutes
Cooking time : 20 minutes

These savouries keep for a long time in an airtight container. A variation is 'kucho nimki' (small nimki) where, after rolling out the dough into a thin circle, it is cut into small pieces with a knife and deep fried.

INGREDIENTS

Flour	~	*250 g*
Salt	~	*½ tsp*
Nigella	~	*1 tsp*
Lime juice	~	*1 tbsp*
Refined oil	~	*for frying*

- Stir the flour with salt. Rub in 2 tablespoons of oil.
- Add the nigella and mix into a semi-soft dough with cold water and lime juice.

- Knead well till it smooth and elastic.
- Divide it into 10 portions.
- Roll out into thin puris with the help of a little oil.
- Fold into halves and then once again fold to form a triangle.
- Press lightly with the rolling pin once.
- Heat enough oil in a karahi and fry 2 to 3 nimkis at a time till a very light brown.
- Tastes equally good hot or at room temperature.

Mochar Chop

Banana Flower Kababs

MAKES 20

Preparation time : 30 minutes
Cooking time : 30 minutes

Instructions on how to cut and clean the banana flower:

The cutting of 'mocha' or banana flower is an art. Before you begin, grease your palms with a little oil. Remove the outer petals and take the small bunch of flowers. You will find a transparent petal at the base of each flower and a white match-like stick. Discard hem. Now, take a bunch of flowers and cut them into very small pieces. Soak them in water for at least 15 minutes.

INGREDIENTS

Medium banana flowers	~	*2*	*Ginger*	~	*50 g*
Turmeric	~	*½ tsp*	*Garlic*	~	*4 cloves*
Bengal gram dal	~	*100 g*	*Onion*	~	*1*

Coriander leaves	~	*1 bunch*	*Peppercorns*	~	*10*
Green chillies	~	*2*	*Egg*	~	*1*
Dry red chillies	~	*2*	*Lime juice*	~	*1 tsp*
Green cardamom	~	*4*	*Salt*	~	*to taste*
Mace	~	*1 petal*	*Refined oil*	~	*for frying*
Poppy seeds	~	*2 tbsp*			

- Clean and cut the banana flowers according to the directions.
- Finely chop the onion, green chillies and coriander leaves. Mix with lime juice. Set aside.
- Pressure cook the banana flowers with turmeric for 7–8 minutes. Strain.
- Cook the Bengal gram dal, chopped ginger, garlic, red chillies, cardamom, mace, poppy seeds, peppercorns and salt together using very little water. Dry up excess liquid, if any.
- Squeeze the cooked banana flower to remove all moisture. Grind along with the gram dal mixture to a smooth paste.
- Beat the egg and mix with the paste. Divide it into 20 balls. Stuff each with a little onion mixture; shape into kababs.
- Heat enough oil in a karahi for deep frying. Fry the kababs, 4 at a time, tilll golden.
- Serve with a chutney or tomato ketchup.

Sweets

Bhapa Sandesh (Steamed Sandesh)

Bhapa Doi (Steamed Yoghurt)

Mishti Doi (Sweet Curd)

Elojhelo Gaja (Fried Flour Sweet)

Rosogolla (Rasgulla)

Notun Gurer Sandesh (Date-Palm Jaggery Sandesh)

Roshomalai (Rasmalai)

(Continues. . .)

Gokul Pithe (Coconut Sweet)

Manikbhog (Sweet Parwal)

Chhanar Payesh (Paneer Kheer)

Lady Kenny (Dark Gulab Jamun)

Chandrapuli (Moulded Coconut Sandesh)

Doodh Puli (Steamed Dumplings in Kheer)

Narkol Nadu (Coconut Balls)

Malpoa (Malpua)

Muger Puli (Fried Mung Dal Sweet)

Kucho Gaja (Small Fried Flour Bits)

(Continues. . .)

Cham Cham (Paneer Ovals in Syrup)

Khirer Tokti (Khoya Squares)

Alootua (Sweet Potato Gulab Jamun)

Palo (Rice Flour Fudge)

Chandranan (Kheer and Coconut Balls in Syrup)

Chanar Bara (Fried Paneer Balls in Syrup)

Sujir Nadu (Semolina Balls)

Nikhutir Payesh (Paneer and Khoya Balls in Kheer)

Tilkuto (Sesame Seed Burfi)

Bhapa Sandesh

Steamed Sandesh

MAKES 15

Preparation time : 30 minutes
Cooking time : 15 minutes

You definitely need homemade paneer for this sweet. Fresh paneer made with lime juice needs no other essence.

INGREDIENTS

Milk	~	*2 lt*
Lime juice	~	*2 tbsp*
Sugar	~	*200 g*
Thick unsweetened kheer	~	*200 g*

- Boil the milk. Add the lime juice. The milk will curdle and separate into whey.
- Strain and hang up in a muslin cloth till all the whey drains out. This will give you a soft paneer.
- Mix paneer, sugar and kheer in a blender.
- Pour into a greased container.

- Cover with aluminium foil.
- Steam in a pressure cooker for 15 minutes.
- Let the pressure come down on its own.
- Take out; cut into pieces.
- Chill and serve.

Bhapa Doi

Steamed Yogurt

SERVES 8

Preparation time	:	1 hour + 2 hours for hanging curd
Cooking time	:	20 minutes

If you don't have the patience or time, use one large tin of condensed milk in place of the kheer; omit sugar in that case.

INGREDIENTS

Curd	~	*750 g*	*Cashewnuts, chopped*	~	*2 tbsp*
Full cream milk	~	*2 lt*	*Raisins*	~	*2 tbsp*
Sugar	~	*250 g*			

- Hang the curd tied in a muslin cloth for 2 hours till most of the whey drains out.
- Cook the milk with sugar till it reduces to ½ a litre. It should be a very thick kheer.

- Blend the curd and kheer together. Use the blender or a hand-held electric beater. Mix the cashewnuts and raisins.
- Lightly oil a mould. Pour in the curd mixture. Cover with aluminium foil.
- Steam for 20 minute in a pressure cooker.
- Unmould; chill and serve decorated with more nuts, if desired.

Mishti Doi

Sweet Curd

SERVES 6–8

Preparation time : 1 hour
Cooking time : Overnight

'Mishti doi' or sweet curd has won many a heart including that of celebrities like cricketer, Sunil Gavaskar. It can be very easily made at home. This curd sets best in an earthen bowl which imparts a delicious fragrance of its own. If you can't procure one, use any other pot.

INGREDIENTS

Cow's milk	~	*800 ml*	*Jaggery, grated*	~	*50 g*
Buffalo's milk	~	*200 ml*	*Curd*	~	*4 tbsp*
Sugar	~	*150 g*			

- Boil both kinds of milk together, stirring well for 20 minutes.
- Add sugar and continue boiling for 15 minutes more.

- Lower the heat and add the jaggery. Stir till it melts. Cool to lukewarm.
- Whip the curd with a little milk and stir thoroughly into the rest of the milk.
- Pour into an earthen bowl.
- Cover well and keep it overnight in a warm draught-free place. During winter, cover the bowl with a woollen shawl.
- If you can't get buffalo's milk, use another 200 ml of cow's milk.

Elojhelo Gaja

Fried Flour Sweet

MAKES 20

Preparation time : 30 minutes
Cooking time : 20 minutes

This keeps well for a fortnight in an airtight container.

INGREDIENTS

Sugar	~	*250 g*	*Ghee*	~	*3 tbsp*
Water	~	*4 tbsp*	*Refined oil*	~	*2 cups*
Flour	~	*250 g*			

- Boil the sugar and water and prepare a syrup of 2-thread consistency. That is, a little syrup stretched between the thumb and forefinger should form 2 threads.
- Mix the flour and ghee together.
- Knead to a semi-hard dough. Knead very well till smooth and elastic.
- Divide it into even sized balls.

- Roll out into thin puris about 7.5 cm in diameter.
- Make a few slits in the centre, taking care that the ends are intact.
- Gather the ends together and press to seal. The middle portion should remain loose and the cuts should show.
- Heat oil in a karahi. Deep fry these "gajas" a few at a time till they are a light golden.
- Dip the fried gajas in syrup. Let them remain for 2 minutes.
- Take them out and keep aside to dry.

Variation: Make small nimkis and prepare kucho gaja (small gaja) in the same way.

Rosogolla

Rasgulla

MAKES 20

Preparation time : 2 hours
Cooking time : 30 minutes

As Bengal's best emissary after Rabindranath Tagore and Satyajit Ray, the rosogolla needs no introduction. The tinned variety has conquered the world.

INGREDIENTS

Cow's milk	~	*1 lt*	*Water*	~	*6½ cups*
Citric acid	~	*½ tsp*	*Sugar*	~	*2 cups*
Flour	~	*1 tsp*	*Rose water*	~	*1 tsp*

- The milk must only be unadulterated cow's milk. No other milk will do. Bring it to a boil.
- Remove from the heat once it comes to a boil and cool. Refrigerate for 8–10 hours. Remove the malai (cream) from the top.

- Mix citric acid with 1 teacup of water.
- Put the milk on the heat again. Remove as soon as it comes to a boil.
- Add the citric acid water, a little at a time, till the milk curdles. You may not need the whole of the citric acid water.
- Drain the paneer and tie loosely in a thin muslin cloth. Place in cold water for half an hour.
- Then hang the paneer up for 1 hour.
- Mash the paneer well. Add the flour and knead to a smooth mixture.
- Divide it into 20 portions. Roll into smooth, crack-free balls.
- Heat the sugar and water in a large vessel like a degchi. Remember, rosogollas puff up to 4 times their original volume.
- When the sugar dissolves and the syrup starts to boil, add the paneer balls gently, one by one.
- Boil uncovered for 5 minutes.
- Cover and cook for 15 minutes, sprinkling a handful of water every 3 minutes. This is done so that the syrup does not thicken. The water must boil continuously.
- When done, the rosogollas will puff up and float to the surface.
- Remove from heat; cool and add rose water.

Notun Gurer Sandesh

Date-Palm Jaggery Sandesh

MAKES 10–12

Preparation time : 10 minutes
Cooking time : 30 minutes

One of the all-time favourites of those who have a sweet tooth is the notun gur or the date-palm jaggery. This jaggery is seasonal and available from late November to February. The date tree is tapped and the juice collected. This juice is boiled to make thin as well as solid jaggery and used in sweets. It is also delicious eaten by itself. It is called 'patali' in Bengali.

INGREDIENTS

Cow's milk	~	*2 lt*	*Solid date-palm jaggery, grated*	~	*6 tbsp*
Sugar	~	*2 tbsp*			

- You don't have to remove the cream from the milk for sandesh. Prepare paneer straight away, using lime juice or citric acid water.
- Let the paneer sit in its water for half an hour. Then strain and hang the paneer up in a muslin cloth for half-an-hour to one hour.
- Mix the paneer with sugar and patali in a karahi over medium heat, stirring constantly.
- The paneer will give out some water. When the moisture dries up a little, reduce the heat and cook, stirring all the while.
- Cook till all but 2 tablespoons of moisture are left. Remove and let it cool.
- Grind in a mixer or on a clean grinding stone till smooth.
- Shape and serve.

Roshomalai

Rasmalai

SERVES 10

Preparation time : 5 minutes
Cooking time : 50 minutes

Next to rosogollas, this is the most popular Bengali sweet outside Bengal.

INGREDIENTS

Milk	~	*2 lt + ¼ lt*	*Water*	~	*¼ lt*
Sugar	~	*150 g*	*Chopped nuts*	~	*2 tbsp*
Rosogollas	~	*20*			

- Boil 2 litres of milk with sugar and reduce to half. Reserve.
- Take out the rosogollas from syrup. Squeeze gently to drain out as much of the syrup as possible without damaging the rosogollas.
- Mix water and ¼ litre of milk. Put to boil.

- As soon as it comes to a boil, put 4–5 rosogollas at a time and boil for 5 minutes. Take them out and keep aside. Repeat and boil all rosogollas this way.
- Put the rosogollas in the thickened milk and simmer for 2–3 minutes.
- Chill and serve garnished with nuts.

Gokul Pithe

Coconut Sweet

MAKES 25–30

Preparation time : 1 hour
Cooking time : 45 minutes

Winter is pithe time in Bengal. 'Pithes' are sweets made of coconut, 'patali gur' (date palm jaggery), sugar, milk, paneer, khoya, rice flour, semolina, etc. Some are even made of dals. Pithes are not sold; they are invariably homemade.

INGREDIENTS

Sugar	~	*500 g*
Water	~	*2½ cups*
Milk	~	*1 lt*
Ghee	~	*1 tbsp*
Coconut, grated	~	*2 large*
Jaggery	~	*4 tbsp*
Cardamom powder	~	*½ tsp*
Ghee or refined oil	~	*as needed*

For the batter:

Flour	~	*250 g*
Milk	~	*¾ cup*
Baking powder	~	*1 tsp*
Salt	~	*a pinch*

- Heat the sugar and water together. Stir until sugar dissolves completely.
- Boil till the syrup attains one-thread consistency, which means, if you take a drop of syrup between your thumb and forefinger and pull the fingers apart, the syrup should form a single thread. Keep the syrup aside.
- Heat ghee in a karahi. Add the grated coconut and fry over a low fire for 2 minutes.
- Add the jaggery and keep stirring, till light brown.
- Add the thickened milk, stir well to mix. Cook for 4–5 minutes, stirring continually.
- Stir in the cardamom powder. Mix well. Remove.
- Now, very lightly grease your hands, take a tablespoon of the coconut mixture and shape it into small tikias.
- Heat enough ghee or oil in a karahi for deep frying. Dip the coconut balls in the batter and deep fry till golden-brown.
- Put them into sugar syrup when they have cooled down a little.
- Keep them immersed in the syrup for a few hours before serving.

For the batter:

- Sieve together the flour, baking powder and salt in a bowl.
- Add all the liquids at once and mix well. The batter should be thick. If necessary, you can add a little more milk.
- Let the batter rest for 20 minutes.

Manikbhog

Sweet Parwal

MAKES 10

Preparation time : 30 minutes
Cooking time : 35 minutes

INGREDIENTS

Parwals (Snake gourd)	~	*10*
Sugar	~	*250 g*
Rose water	~	*1 tbsp*
Khoya	~	*1 cup*
Powdered sugar	~	*2 tbsp*
Pistachios, chopped	~	*2 tbsp*
Almonds, chopped	~	*2 tbsp*
Cardamom powder	~	*½ tsp*
Silver leaf	~	*10*

- Wash, peel and slit the parwals from one side. Carefully remove the seeds and pith.
- Boil water in a large pan. Add the parwals and cook until just tender. Drain well.
- Pierce each parwal a few times with a fork.
- Boil the sugar with 1 cup of water and 1 teaspoon of lime juice for 10 minutes. Strain.

- Put the syrup on the heat again. Add the cooked parwals and rose water and simmer on a very slow fire for 10 minutes. By this time, the parwals will look opaque.
- Remove; let the extra syrup drain out. Cool.
- In the meantime, lightly fry the khoya in a karahi without oil.
- Add the powdered sugar and mix well. Add the nuts and cool.
- Stuff each parwal with the khoya mixture.
- Decorate with silver foil.

Chhanar Payesh

Paneer Kheer

SERVES 6

Preparation time : 5 minutes
Cooking time : 35 minutes

INGREDIENTS

Paneer	~	*250 g*
Milk	~	*2 lt*
Sugar	~	*250 g*
Cashewnuts	~	*1 tbsp*
Chironji	~	*1 tbsp*

- Cut the paneer into small cubes.
- Boil the milk. When reduced to half, add the sugar.
- Boil for 5 minutes more.
- Add the paneer cubes and boil for another 10 minutes.
- Remove from heat
- Serve cold in a china bowl decorated with nuts.

Lady Kenny

Dark Gulab Jamun

MAKES 12

Preparation time : 20 minutes + reservation time

Cooking time : 30 minutes

INGREDIENTS

Khoya	~	*2 cups*	*Sugar*	~	*3 cups*
Paneer	~	*2 cups*	*Pistachios*	~	*12*
Milk	~	*⅓ cup*	*Cardamom powder*	~	*1 tsp*
Semolina	~	*½ cups*	*Ghee*	~	*for deep frying*
Baking powder	~	*½ tsp*			

- Mix the khoya, paneer, semolina and baking powder together.
- Sprinkle a little milk and knead well to form a soft and smooth dough. Keep it aside for 2 hours.

- Boil the sugar with 1½ cups of water till the syrup reaches a one-thread consistency.
- Add the cardamom powder and remove from fire.
- Divide the khoya mixture into 12 portions. Stuff a pistachio into each part. Roll them into smooth round balls.
- Heat ghee in a karahi. Take off the heat and put in a few balls at a time.
- Turn on the heat again and fry over low heat till the balls turn dark brown.
- Drain and put them into the syrup.
- Serve hot or at room temperature.

Chandrapuli

Moulded Coconut Sandesh

MAKES 25

Preparation time : 30 minutes
Cooking time : 20 minutes

Moulds for chandrapulis are special ones. These are half-moon shaped with intricate designs and comes in various sizes.

INGREDIENTS

Coconut	~	*1 large*	*Sugar*	~	*250 g*
Paneer	~	*250 g*	*Ghee*	~	*1 tbsp*
Khoya	~	*250 g*	*Cardamom powder*	~	*1 tsp*

- Grate coconut and grind till smooth.
- Grind together the ground coconut, paneer and khoya in the mixer till well mixed. No water is to be added. A grinding stone may be used instead to mix the ingredients.

- Combine the coconut mixture, sugar and ghee in a karahi and put on medium heat.
- Cook, stirring constantly, while at the same time pressing the mixture against the sides of the karahi with a heavy ladle.
- Stir till the mixture leaves the sides of the karahi. Add the cardamom powder and remove.
- When cool enough to touch, divide it into 25 parts.
- Press each part against a greased mould evenly and you'll get the shape. Prepare all the chandrapulis the same way. It keeps for at least a week even outside a refrigerator.

Doodh Puli

Steamed Dumplings in Kheer

MAKES 12–15

Preparation time : 20 minutes
Cooking time : 20 minutes

INGREDIENTS

Coconut	~	*½*	*Milk*	~	*3 cups*
Sugar or jaggery	~	*100 g*	*Patali gur*	~	*100 g*
Semolina	~	*1 cup, heaped*	*Cardamom powder*	~	*½ tsp*

- Grate the coconut. Add sugar or jaggery and stir over medium heat till well mixed and soft. Remove.
- Add 1½ cups of water to the semolina and let it cook over medium heat, stirring all the while.

- When the semolina soaks up the water and leaves the sides of the karahi, remove. It should be soft.
- When cool enough to touch, divide it into 12–15 balls.
- Stuff each ball with a little coconut filling and shape into tikias.
- Put the milk to boil. Add patali gur and stir till it dissolves.
- Add the semolina tikias carefully.
- Cook for 5 minutes on low heat. Remove.
- It can be served warm or chilled.

Narkol Nadu

Coconut Balls

MAKES 30

Preparation time : 25 minutes
Cooking time : 20 minutes

Like in South India, coconut trees abound in Bengal too. Hence, it is extensively used in both savoury and sweet dishes. There are innumerable varieties of coconut sweets. These nadus are the most popular. You can use 'gur' or jaggery in place of sugar. The 'nadus' in that case will be dark brown.

INGREDIENTS

Coconut, grated	~	*4 cups*	*Milk powder*	~	*½ cup*
Sugar	~	*3 cups*	*Cardamom powder*	~	*1 tsp*

- Grind the coconut and put in a karahi with the sugar.
- Keep stirring. The sugar will give out some water and mix with the coconut.
- When quite thick, add the milk powder.

- Keep on stirring till the mixture leaves the sides of the karahi. Remove.
- Add the cardamom powder.
- When the mixture is cool enough to touch, grease your palms and shape it into balls.

Variation: Camphor powder can be added instead of cardamom powder. And very thick unsweetened kheer or khoya can replace milk powder.

Malpoa

Malpua

MAKES 25

Preparation time : 10 minutes + soaking
Cooking time : 40 minutes

INGREDIENTS

Semolina	~	*150 g*	*Aniseed*	~	*2 tsp*
Flour	~	*250 g*	*Garam masala powder*	~	*1 pinch*
Sugar	~	*200 g*	*Ghee or refined oil*	~	*for frying*
Peppercorns, roughly crushed	~	*10*			

- Soak the semolina in 2 cups of water for half-an-hour.
- Mix the soaked semolina with all the other ingredients except the oil.
- Add enough water to make a batter of pouring consistency.
- Pour enough ghee or oil in a karahi. If using refined oil, add 1 tablespoon of ghee for extra flavour. This is, however, optional.

- Pour ¼ cupful of batter and deep fry one malpua at a time.
- Turn over and fry the other side, too. The malpuas shoul be a light golden in colour.
- Drain and serve hot or cold. These keep well for a few days.

Muger Puli

Fried Mung Dal Sweet

MAKES 20

Preparation time : 50 minutes
Cooking time : 30 minutes

INGREDIENTS

Mung dal	~	*250 g*	*Coconut, grated*	~	*1½ cups*
Salt	~	*1 pinch*	*Patali gur*	~	*100 g*
Semolina	~	*75 g*	*Ghee or oil*	~	*for deep frying*

- Roast the mung dal in a dry karahi, stirring well till the dal starts to pick up brown spots and you get a lovely aroma.
- Remove and wash the dal well. Boil in a degchi till just done. Strain. Do not use a pressure cooker as the dal will get overcooked.
- Knead the strained dal, adding salt and semolina, into a dough. Keep covered.

- For the filling, cook coconut and grated patali gur together on medium heat in a karahi. Stir well till well mixed and soft.
- Divide the dal and coconut mixture into 20 portions each.
- Stuff one part of the filling into one part of the dal mixture and prepare sausage-shaped pulis.
- Heat enough oil or ghee in a karahi for deep frying. Fry the pulis, a few at a time, till golden. Remove.
- It tastes equally good hot or cold.

Kucho Gaja

Small Fried Flour Bits

SERVES 10–12

Preparation time : 30 minutes
Cooking time : 30 minutes

INGREDIENTS

Flour	~	*250 g*	*Soda bicarbonate*	~	*a pinch*
Ghee	~	*2½ tbsp*	*Refined oil*	~	*for deep frying*
Sugar	~	*300 g*			

- Make a syrup of 3-thread consistency with the sugar and half-a-cup of water.
- Sieve the flour and soda together. Rub in the ghee well. Add enough water to make a sticky dough.
- Knead for 10 minutes or till the dough is smooth and elastic.

- Divide the dough into 5 portions
- Roll out each portion like a thick chapatti. Prick each a few times with a fork.
- Now, with a sharp knife, cut the chapattis into long strips of 2.5 cm each. Again, cut them horizontally the same way.
- You will now have several small pieces. Keep them aside.
- Heat enough oil for deep frying in a karahi. When it begins to smoke, take off the heat. Add as many pieces of the dough as the karahi will hold comfortably. Fry till light golden. Remove.
- Dip fried gajas in syrup. Let them soak for one minute.
- Take out and keep aside to dry. Keeps well for at least a fortnight.

Cham Cham

Paneer Ovals in Syrup

MAKES 10

Preparation time : 30 minutes
Cooking time : 20 minutes

INGREDIENTS

Cow's milk	~	*1 lt*	*Flour*	~	*1¼ tsp*
Sugar	~	*2 cups*	*Rose water*	~	*1 tbsp*
Water	~	*7 cups*			

- Prepare paneer from the milk as for rosogollas.
- Put the sugar and water to boil. Stir till sugar dissolves.
- Add 1 tablespoon of lime juice and boil for 2 minutes. You'll find the scum rising to the surface. Strain the syrup and keep it aside.
- Knead the paneer till soft. Add the flour and knead again till well mixed and smooth.
- Divide the paneer mixture into 10 equal parts and shape them into flat ovals.

- Put the strained syrup to boil again in a degchi.
- When it comes to a boil again, add the cham chams carefully.
- Boil for 8 minutes, sprinkling a handful of water twice in between.
- Now, partly cover the vessel and boil for another 5 minutes. Sprinkle 1 tablespoon of water once.
- Take off the fire. Let the cham chams soak in the syrup for four hours.
- Sprinkle rose water and serve.

Khirer Tokti

Khoya Squares

SERVES 8

Preparation time : 5 minutes
Cooking time : 15 minutes

INGREDIENTS

Khoya	~	*500 g*	*Meetha itar*	~	*2 drops*
Sugar	~	*300 g*	*Silver leaf*	~	*for decoration*

- Grate the khoya and powder sugar.
- Combine the khoya and sugar and place on medium heat in a karahi.
- Cook, stirring continuously, till thick. But the mixture should remain moist.
- Mix meetha itar with 2 teaspoons of water and add it to the khoya. Mix well.
- Pour evenly on a greased plate.
- Decorate with silver leaf.
- Cut into diamond-shaped pieces and serve.
- A handful of chopped almonds may be added.

Alootua

Sweet Potato Gulab Jamun

MAKES 24

Preparation time : 40 minutes
Cooking time : 30 minutes

INGREDIENTS

Sweet potatoes	~	*2 kg*
Flour	~	*2 tbsp*
Khoya	~	*150 g*
Cardamom powder	~	*1 tsp*
Sugar	~	*2 cups*
Water	~	*1 cup*
Ghee or refined oil	~	*for deep frying*

- Boil and peel the sweet potatoes. Mash well, discarding fibres, if any.
- Add the flour and knead into a smooth dough. Divide it into 24 portions.
- Heat 1 teaspoon of ghee in a karahi. Add the grated khoya and stir fry till light brown.
- Add the powdered cardamom and remove. Divide into 24 parts.

- Take one part of sweet potato, fill with one part of khoya, and roll it into a smooth ball. Prepare all other balls the same way.
- Boil the sugar and water together till the syrup reaches a one-thread consistency. Keep aside.
- Heat enough ghee or refined oil in a karahi for deep frying.
- Fry the sweet potato balls, a few at a time, over a low medium heat till golden.
- Drop them in the sugar syrup and keep overnight.
- These sweet potato gulab jamuns are very soft, so handle them carefully.

Palo

Rice Flour Fudge

SERVES 8–10

Preparation time : 45 minutes
Cooking time : 45 minutes

INGREDIENTS

Rice	~	*2 cups*	*Milk*	~	*1 lt*
Sugar	~	*1 cup*	*Cashewnuts, broken*	~	*½ cup*
Date palm jaggery	~	*300 g*	*Raisins*	~	*10*
Green cardamom powder	~	*1 tsp*	*Coconut, grated*	~	*½ cup*
Bay leaves	~	*4*			

- Grind the rice to a powder in a blender.
- Mix the rice powder with 2 litres of water and put on heat. Let it boil. Cook, stirring constantly.

- About 20 minutes later, when the mixture thickens somewhat, add the rest of the ingredients.
- Stir carefully. This mixture has a tendency to splutter. Use a long-handled spoon.
- Remove when the mixture becomes quite thick, like porridge. Remove the bay leaves.
- Grease a tray and evenly spread the mixture on it.
- Refrigerate when cool.
- Cut and serve.

Chandranan

Kheer and Coconut Balls in Syrup

MAKES 35–40

Preparation time : 30 minutes
Cooking time : 30 minutes

INGREDIENTS

Coconut	~	*1 large*	*Ghee or oil*	~	*for deep frying*
Khoya	~	*250 g*	*Sugar*	~	*300 g*
Semolina	~	*6 tbsp*			

- Grate the coconut and khoya; grind together in a mixer without water till smooth.
- Put on medium heat in a karahi. Cook, stirring, till well mixed and the mixture leaves the sides of the karahi.
- Add the semolina. Stir to mix well and remove. Keep aside till lukewarm.

- Divide into 35–40 small balls and shape them like tikias. Let them cool.
- Heat oil or ghee in a karahi and deep fry the cold tikias, a few at a time. Do not fry while the tikias are still hot, or they will break.
- Prepare a syrup with sugar and 1 cup of water till it reaches a one-thread consistency.
- Put the fried coconut tikias into the syrup.
- Serve after an hour.

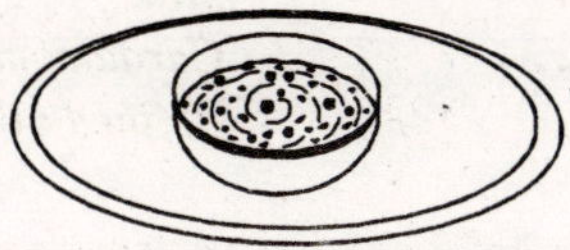

Chanar Bara

Fried Paneer Balls in Syrup

MAKES 20–25

Preparation time : 30 minutes
Cooking time : 25 minutes

This is an economic version of the gulab jamun.

INGREDIENTS

Sugar	~	*500 g*	*Ghee*	~	*1 tbsp*
Water	~	*2 cups*	*Milk*	~	*2 cups*
Paneer	~	*125 g*	*Cardamom powder*	~	*½ tsp*
Flour	~	*250 g*	*Refined oil*	~	*for deep frying*

- Put the sugar and water to boil. Let it cook till the syrup reaches one-thread consistency, which means, if a little syrup is stretched between the thumb and index finger it should form a thread.
- The paneer should preferably be made at home. Hang the paneer tied in a muslin cloth till all the whey drains out.
- Mash the paneer till smooth.
- Mix the ghee with flour.
- Mix milk with flour, a little at a time. Add 1½ cups milk to begin with.
- Add the kneaded paneer and mix well. The batter should be thick like pakoda batter. Add the remaining milk only if necessary.
- Finally, add the cardamom powder.
- Heat enough oil in a karahi for deep frying.
- Drop spoonfuls of batter and fry till they are golden. You'll have to do this in batches.
- Take out the paneer balls and put them in the sugar syrup.
- Let them soak for at least 2 hours before serving.

Sujir Nadu

Semolina Balls

MAKES 20

Preparation time : 10 minutes
Cooking time : 30 minutes

INGREDIENTS

Ghee	~	*6 tbsp*	*Sugar*	~	*350 g*
Semolina	~	*½ kg*	*Raisins*	~	*20*
Coconut	~	*½*	*Cardamom powder*	~	*½ tsp*

- Heat ghee in a karahi and then remove from the heat.
- Add the semolina. Stir fry for a minute and put on medium heat again.
- Stir continually till the semolina is golden brown.
- Add grated coconut and fry for another 3–4 minutes. Remove.
- Boil sugar in ¾ cup of water till it reaches a one-thread consistency.

- Add the syrup to semolina along with the raisins and powdered cardamom. Mix well.
- Cover semolina with a tight lid and keep for an hour.
- Uncover; stir to mix well once more, and break up lumps, if any.
- Shape into small lime-sized balls.
- When completely cooled, store in airtight containers. These taste better after a day.

Nikhutir Payesh

Paneer and Khoya Balls in Kheer

SERVES 8

Preparation time : 25 minutes
Cooking time : 45 minutes

INGREDIENTS

Khoya	~	*250 g*	*Sugar*	~	*400 g*
Flour	~	*2 tbsp*	*Cardamom powder*	~	*½ tsp*
Ghee	~	*½ cup*	*Rose water*	~	*1 tsp*
Milk	~	*2 lt*			

- The khoya must be of the soft variety. Knead the khoya and flour together till it is smooth and no lumps remain.
- Divide the mixture into 50 very small parts and shape into ovals.
- Heat ghee in a karahi. Remove from heat and add the khoya balls. Stir and put on medium heat again.

- Fry, stirring, till it turns a light brown. Remove after straining the ghee well. Keep it aside.
- Combine the milk and sugar; put on heat in a degchi.
- Cook, stirring, till the milk is reduced to half.
- Carefully stir in the fried khoya balls and cook over low heat for 5 minutes.
- Add the cardamom powder and rose water and remove.
- Chill and serve.

Tilkuto

Sesame Seed Burfi

SERVES 8

Preparation time : 20 minutes
Cooking time : 20 minutes

INGREDIENTS

Sesame seeds	~	*250 g*	*Sugar*	~	*400 g*
Paneer	~	*250 g*	*Cardamom powder*	~	*½ tsp*
Khoya	~	*250 g*			

- Pick and clean the sesame seeds. Do not wash.
- Heat a karahi and put in sesame seeds. Remove from heat and stir continuously for a minute.
- Place over medium low heat again and stir continuously.
- Remove when the seeds just start to pop, but continue stirring even when off the heat or the seeds will burn.
- Let it cool and grind in it the mixer to get a coarse powder.

- Grind the paneer and khoya together and combine with sugar.
- Put on heat and stir like the sandesh. A lot of moisture will be given out.
- Add the sesame-seed powder and cardamom powder. Mix well.
- Cook for 1–2 minutes, stirring all the while.
- Remove while still quite moist.
- Pour evenly onto a greased plate.
- Cut and serve when cold.

Glossary

CONDIMENTS AND NUTS

ENGLISH	HINDI	ENGLISH	HINDI	ENGLISH	HINDI
Allspice	*Kababchini*	Coconut, dry	*Copra*	Jaggery (molasses)	*Gur*
Aniseed	*Saunf*	Coconut, fresh	*Nariel*	Lemon rind	*Nimbu ka chilka*
Arrowroot	*Araroht*	Coriander leaves	*Hara dhania*	Mace	*Javitri*
Asafoetida	*Hing*	Coriander seeds	*Sookha dhania*	Mango Powder	*Amchur*
Baking Power	*Khane ka soda*	Cumin	*Jeera*	Melon seeds	*Magaj*
Bay Leaf	*Tejpatta*	Curry leaves	*Curry patta/ Meetha neem ke patte*	Mint leaves	*Pudina*
Black pepper or peppercorns	*Kali mirch*	Dry pome-granate seeds	*Anardana, Sookhi*	Mustard seeds	*Sarson or Rai*
Breadcrumbs	*Sukhi double roti ka choora*	Fennel	*Saunf*	Nutmeg	*Jaiphal*
Caraway seeds	*Shahjeera*	Fenugreek	*Methi/ Kasuri methi*	Onion seeds	*Kalonji*
Cardamoms	*Elaichi*	Garlic	*Lasan*	Pistachio	*Pista*
Cashewnuts	*Kaju*	Ginger, fresh	*Adrak*	Poppy seeds	*Khus khus*
Cinnamon	*Dalchini*	Ginger, dry	*Sonth*	Raisins	*Kishmish*
Cloves	*Laung*	Green chillies	*Hari mirch*	Red Chillies	*Lal mirch*
Coconut, desiccated	*Sukha nariel ka choora*	Groundnuts	*Moongphalli*	Rose Water	*Gulab jal*
				Saffron	*Zafran/ Kesar*

ENGLISH	HINDI
Sesame seed	*Til*
Star Anise	*Chakriphool*
Sultanas	*Munakka*
Tamarind	*Imli*
Turmeric	*Haldi*
Thymol seeds	*Ajwain*
Vinegar	*Sirka*
Vetivier	*Kewra*
Fruits	
Apples	*Seb*
Apricots	*Khubani*
Banana	*Kela*
Fig	*Anjeer*
Grapes	*Angoor*
Lemon	*Meetha nimbu*
Lime	*Nimbu*
Mango	*Aam*
Orange	*Narangi or Santra*
Peaches	*Aadoo*
Pears	*Nashpati*
Pineapple	*Anaras*
Pomegranate	*Anar*
Papaya	*Papita*
Sweet Lime	*Musambi*
Vegetables	
Beetroot	*Chukandar*
Brinjal (Eggplant, aubergine)	*Baingan*
Cabbage	*Band gobhi*
Capsicum	*Shimla mirch*
Carrot	*Gajar*
Cauliflower	*Phool gobhi*
Cucumber	*Kheera*
Fenugreek Leaves	*Methi ke patte*
French beans	*Phras bean*
Green Peas	*Matar*
Mushrooms	*Gucchi*
Onions	*Pyaz*
Potatoes	*Aloo*
Pumpkin	*Kaddu*
Spinach	*Palak*
Spring Onions	*Hara pyaz*
Tomato	*Tamatar*
Turnip	*Shalgam*
White Gourd	*Lauki*
Lentils and Cereals	
Bengal gram	*Chana dal*
Black gram	*Udad dal*
Corn	*Makkai*
Flour	*Maida*
Wholemeal flour	*Atta*
Green gram	*Moong dal*
Gram flour	*Besan*
Large White gram	*Kabulichana*
Lentil	*Masur dal*
Red gram	*Arhar dal*
Rice	*Chawal*
Sago	*Sabudana*
Semolina	*Suji*
Wheat	*Genhu*
Cracked Wheat	*Dalia*
Puffed rice	*Murmura*
Pressed rice	*Chiwda or Poha*

Glossary of Bengali Terms

Alur chop	A kind of fried potato cake made by dipping balls of spiced mashed potatoes in batter and deep-frying in oil.
Bara/bora	Round balls of fish or vegetables, usually deep-fried.
Bhat	Plain boiled rice.
Bori	Small pellets of ground, spiced dal, dried in the sun and stored throughout the year, to be used in stews and vegetable preparations.
Chhana	The solid part of milk curdled by the addition of acid.
Chholar dal	Yellow split peas.
Chingri	A generic term denoting all kinds of shrimps and prawns.
Chitol	A large fish, prized especially by the people of East Bengal, with a very soft oily stomach or frontal portion, and a very bony back portion.
Dab	The green coconut.
Daga	The bony back portion of the fish.
Dhonka	Dhonkas are made out of ground, pressed dal to form squares.
Doi	Yoghurt.
Gur	Indigenous sugar.
Halua	Sweet dish made with cream of wheat, eggs, flour and other things in ghee and sugar.
Handi	A cooking pot with a rounded bottom, slightly narrowed at the neck with a wide rim to facilitate holding. Rice is traditionally cooked in a handi.
Ilish	The Bengali name for hilsa.

Jalkhabar	Usually a light afternoon snack, the equivalent of the English tea.
Jhola gur	Liquid gur, made by boiling the sap from the date-palm tree.
Kachchi biryani	A Muslim preparation where uncooked rice and meat are cooked together over a very low flame.
Kachu	Any of several kinds of colocasia.
Kachu shak	The stems, not leaves of colocasia, eaten as a vegetable.
Kachuri	A stuffed fried bread.
Kalai dal	A kind of pulse very popular among the people of West Bengal.
Kalo jeera	Literally, black cumin. Sometimes called onion seeds in English.
Karai	A cooking pot, shaped like a Chinese wok, but much deeper, used for deep frying.
Karola	The larger variety of bitter gourd.
Kasundi	A sour mustard pickle, usually made in the summer, eaten with rice and fried vegetables.
Katla	One of the several kinds of freshwater carp.
Kheer	Evaporated milk.
Khichuri	Rice and dal cooked together with a variety of spices.
Koi	A kind of fish, served whole, sometimes called a climbing perch.
Kumro	The pumpkin.
Langcha	A kind of sweet, but shaped like a bolster.
Lau	The favourite Bengali gourd, pale green on the outside and white inside.
Luchi	A circular fried bread, either puffy like a balloon or flaky.
Machh	Fish.

Machher jhol	Fish stew.
Magur	A kind of fish of the catfish variety.
Malaikari	A preparation of prawns made with coconut milk.
Malpo	A home-made sweet.
Matar dal	Dal made from green peas.
Matarshuti	Green peas. Matarshutir kachuri has ground green peas as the filling inside the bread.
Mirgel	A smaller variety of carp.
Mishti	Sweet (adjective) or sweets (as a collective noun).
Mishti doi	Sweet yoghurt.
Mocha	Banana blossom.
Muthiya	A term used by the people of East Bengal to denote fish balls made by shaping them in the palm or muthi.
Mulo	The native radish, available during the winter.
Muri	Puffed rice.
Muror dal	A preparation combining roasted moong dal with a muro or fish head and spices.
Narkel	The ripe coconut.
Panch phoron	Literally, five flavours. Usually a combination of five whole spices, cumin, kalo jeera, mustard, fennel and fenugreek.
Papor	The Bengali word for papadam, thin sheets of spiced ground dal, dried in the sun or in an oven, and fried just before serving.
Parota	The Bengali word for paratha. Fried bread, circular or triangular in shape, often with two or three layers, but sometimes more.

Patali gur	The solidified sap of the date-palm tree, made by repeated boilings.
Patishapta	A home-made sweet, like crepes, usually stuffed with ground coconut and khejur gur.
Patol	A small, green gourd-shaped vegetable.
Paturi	Anything cooked wrapped in a leaf (pata) and left over a slow flame or in the embers of a coal stove.
Payesh	Anything, usually rice, cooked in milk.
Peti	The front or stomach portion of a big fish.
Phoron	A flavouring agent. All dals are first boiled in water, then flavoured with a specific combination of spices fried in oil or ghee.
Posto	Poppy seeds.
Raita	A salad of yoghurt and cucumbers.
Rajbhog	A large spherical sweet made with chhana, floating in syrup.
Rasogollas	Perhaps the most famous Bengali sweet. These are balls made with *chhana* and boiled in a plain syrup.
Rasomalai	A kind of sweet with rasogollas floating in sweetened evaporated milk.
Rui	The most prized variety of freshwater carp.
Sandesh	Like the rasogolla, a famous Bengali sweet made with *chhana*.
Shak	Any kind of leafy green, eaten as a vegetable.
Shingara	Triangular flour shells stuffed with vegetables or meat and deep-fried in oil.
Shol	A kind of fish, usually bought live.
Shorshe	Mustard. Hilsa cooked in a mustard sauce is called shorshe ilish.
Shukto	A bitter vegetable dish, served as a first course with rice.
Taal	The fruit of the palm tree.